FROM THE ASHES I RISE

Dare to Do the Impossible

Dr. Mildred Dalton Hampton-Henry

Front Page Publishing, LLC
5198 Arlington Ave
Riverside, CA, 92504

www.frontpagepublishing.com

FROM THE ASHES I RISE

Contents

PART II – THE WESTWARD TREK

PREFACE

As I look back to the sunrise of my youth, I ponder the question, "What footprints did I leave in the sand to be followed?" I have traveled from the cradle to this point on the road of life, navigating many resting stops and fueling spots, and I wonder what guiding road signs have I left. I write this book with much humility, in hopes that I may provide footprints that can be seen in the dark. May it help someone realize that no matter how long and dark the night, the light always comes in the morning.

The inspiration to write this book and preserve history began with seeing the struggles experienced by my people, the records kept by my mother, and the court battles my family faced to preserve the family farm, our history, and our legacy. In American History, many Black families and farms fell by the wayside. The tenacity of my parents and ancestors is amazing. The accomplishments of my immediate family, despite adversities, inspired me.

I meditated on how much of my negative personal experiences to share, realizing that these are the very painful abusive encounters with which someone may be struggling, and could be inspired to overcome. I share my history trusting that the information will be helpful and not derogatory.

A whole list of acclamations would be needed to express my gratitude to my biological and spiritual children, family, and friends who laughed with me, cried with me, and survived many battles with me. The names are too numerous to list here, however, I especially dedicate this book to my parents, Ulysses G. Dalton II, and Alma Rodgers Dalton; to my children: Angelo, Alvia, Delano, Lawrence, and Pamela Hampton; to my spiritual son, Dwaine Radden, Sr. and family; to my brother Dr. U.G. Dalton III, and sisters Velma and Vhaness; and to those who helped edit and prepare the manuscript, such as Tammie Jackson, Mary Welch, and Dr. Jean Peacock.

Thank you for the encouragement I was given and the friendly sharing of helpful information. I am grateful to you, for without you there would be no me. You gave me great inspiration to reach out and touch many lives along my journey. Walk with me now and thank you for taking the time to journey with me as we travel the road that led to somewhere.
If you've any work to do
Do it with all your will;
If you ever reach the top
You'll have to climb the hill.
-Lillian Bowles

My Culture

PART I

IN THE BEGINNING

On a cold February morning in 1933, in Tamo, Arkansas, the hands of a local midwife delivered a squalling baby girl into the world. Incorrectly named Dorothy Ann by the midwife, Mildred Monette Dalton was to be the last child born to the union of Alma Earnestine Rodgers Dalton and Ulysses Grant Dalton, Jr. The baby did not know about the discrepancy until a birth certificate was needed to enter graduate school 45 years later.

A towering water tank, located in the bend of the highway one-half mile north of Dalton's Crossing, identifies the Tamo community for travelers. This tiny community of Arkansas flatlands in the southeastern section of Jefferson County, approximately 65 miles southeast of Little Rock, is a deeply rural farming community mostly a place of fields and woods. The Dalton farm is listed in the Jefferson County Arkansas Courthouse as "The Town of Dalton."

The nearest large town, approximately 19 miles to the north is Pine Bluff, Arkansas. Joseph Bonne, an interpreter for the United States Government at the signing of the Quapaw Cession on August 21, 1818, at St. Louis, Missouri, and his wife, Mary Imbeau, built a log cabin on the first bluff above the mouth of the Arkansas River. Covered with towering pine trees, this settlement was later officially named "The Town of Pine Bluff."

This contiguous Arkansas scene has two focal places, Tamo, my birthplace and homestead, and Pine Bluff, the economic, educational, cultural center, and county seat for Jefferson County. A common social denominator between the two is that both places were segregated. From grade school at Tamo, through Merrill High School in Pine Bluff, through Washington Technical High School in St. Louis, through a college degree at Agricultural, Mechanical, and Normal College in Pine Bluff, I never had a White classmate or teacher. Teachers, coaches, administrators, doctors, lawyers, and professionals were all Black. In short, I was raised in Arkansas' African American communities of pride, progress, and role models, which greatly impacted my loyalties and behaviors throughout my lifetime.

It was a big treat to go to Little Rock, the state's capital, and the closest thing Arkansas has to a major metropolitan city. There was a steep hill on Roosevelt Road, and it took two feet to drive a vehicle on the hill. One foot was kept on the brake to keep from rolling backwards downhill, and the other foot was kept on the accelerator. Mother had two sisters living in Little Rock, Aunt Viola and Aunt Aurola, and their families. Aunt Aurola had four children who were the same ages as Mother's four children. There were visits between the city cousins and country cousins. I was still sucking my thumb at age 13, but upon visiting my city cousins and meeting their male friends, I was embarrassed and ceased the thumb sucking habit. My parents had tried, unsuccessfully, for years to eliminate the habit.

The three sisters, Aunt Viola, Aunt Aurola, and Mother, had a close relationship. Aunt Viola helped rear the younger children when their mother died. My mother's parents, Henry and Lilly Rodgers, were well respected providers for the family. Mother and Uncle Felton were sent to a private school and mother was given piano lessons. Following the death of Grandmother Lilly, Aunt Viola assumed household tasks until years later when Grandfather Henry married Ms. Roxie Mabrey, the only grandmother I knew.

My earliest memories are of the family farming routines. Daddy built a fire in the big wood-burning stove in the living room at dawn, to heat the entire house. Today we turn up the thermostat. Mother began breakfast in the kitchen with aromas permeating the house from the iron stove that had a "warmer" on top, over the surface of the stove, and a space on the right to hold and warm the water. The oven was in the front of the stove, just like today's appliances. Daddy then went outside to meet workers, hitch up the mules, get on the tractor, and immediately begin work in the cool hours of the day. He would later come in briefly for breakfast and return to the fields until the midday meal.

We had two mules named Jeff and Jim, one black and one red. The white pony was called "pony"; she was known to be eccentric and only wanted my father to ride her. The mules pulled the plows and other farm equipment to till the soil.

Before the arsonist burned our store, I can remember Daddy going out of the front door to the store to open up for customers. The store was a wonderment seen through the eyes of a child. Behind the counters were shelves and shelves of items. One side of the store held food items - including counters and display cases of meat, cheese, and other products. On the other side were non-food items. The rear of the store was the business office where Daddy mostly worked, as someone else waited on customers.

Next to the business office was a room that I can only remember being used by women of our community who came with their "scraps" to make quilts. They sewed the pieces together, stretched the bottom cotton pieces on frames; put the cotton/the padding between the colorful top, and the bottom; and meticulously cross-stitched the three sections together, by hand, to make a beautiful creation. The scraps were small odd-shaped pieces of material left from sewing clothes and other items. Many of the clothes were made from colorful sacks in which flour had been purchased. The sacks were washed, cut open, measured, patterns cut, and used to make colorful dresses, skirts, shirts, or whatever the imagination conceived. We had a foot treadle-operated Singer Sewing Machine on which Mother made many of our clothing. This is my first recollection of "recycling." The ladies laughed, sang, told stories, and socialized as they worked. The children that came with the ladies had hours of fun playing "hide and go seek," "Old grey mare, I'll ride him," playing with Chinaberries from the Chinaberry tree; swinging on the big tires hung from tree limbs, and other games.

I remember having few toys with which to play, so we improvised and made our toys. For a boat, we took a block of wood, and a stick, and pushed it down the muddy ditch of water after a rain. The bullfrogs on the bank of the ditch were a choir that provided music for us. Our swing was a car tire hung with ropes from a tree limb. Today, I buy lobster in a restaurant, but as a child, I caught crayfish or crawdads-which looked like pint-size lobsters. We fished in the canal, under the railroad trestle behind my house. After 80 plus years of simply calling the water "The Canal," I was informed in 2021 that the canal had a name, "Wagon Bayou" which flowed an extensive distance.

Crawdads and Bullfrogs were considered "good eating." What a wonderful thing to grab a fishing pole and go fishing for crawdads! The fishing pole was, in reality, a stick with a string tied on the end of it with a piece of wire bent up into the shape of a hook on the end. We would then dig up worms from behind the house and head for the Canal behind the house. The Canal was about ½ block from our back porch, flowed underneath a railroad track. The railroad trestle built to span the Canal was the target area. We could always catch crawdads in the Canal under the trestle.

After catching the crawdads, we pinched off the tail, and the upper body we threw back into the Canal. You see, we were told that the crawdad would grow another tail. The tasty meat was taken from the shell, washed, salt and peppered, and fried for some "sho 'nuff good eating!" I remember this serene setting as a peaceful kingdom in a land of contentment. There was happiness, music, laughter, friendships, industry, and togetherness.

Another interesting food was the bullfrog. The bullfrog was much larger than the toad frog and was edible, almost as a delicacy. Bullfrogs were usually caught on the banks of ditches alongside the roads after it rained. The bullfrog made a loud sound something like a two-level horn. We ate the large legs of the bullfrog, which could propel the bullfrog for yards at each jump. The meat tasted somewhat like chicken or rabbit. I was always fascinated watching the meat cook in the skillet because the meat continued to quiver or jump as it was cooking. Once the meat was fried, however, there was no more movement, just good eating!

In addition to the meat, a menu may consist of purple hull peas cooked with a few pods of okra, fried corn, or corn on the cob, fried okra, sliced tomatoes and cucumbers, cornbread, peach cobbler, and fresh buttermilk, just churned that morning.

Mother was an excellent cook, and food could usually be found cooling on the back porch. Sister Vhaness tells of the time Mother cooked a big goose and had it on the back porch cooling as she prepared the dressing and other food. Upon her return, the goose was gone! Mother was "hot as a firecracker," but no one ever admitted knowing anything about that goose. Hobos traveling the railroad track sometimes came to the back door for food. Unable to locate the guilty goose thieves, and to escape Mother's wrath, the poor hobos were blamed for the missing goose.

Since we lived in a rural area, everybody worked. Each of the four siblings was assigned a cow for which we were responsible. We had to milk the cow, feed it, and tend to the needs of the animal. Cows were milked each morning, before school, so there was always fresh milk to drink. We also had to feed the chickens, feed the hogs, clean the house, and perform other chores before and after school.

Making buttermilk is a process that has faded with the arrival of automation; a process that took place with the additional milk that we did not consume. We sat the milk out "on the back porch" until the milk became "clabber" - a congealed state, and the cream "rose to the top" of the milk. When the cream rose to the top of the milk, all was put in a churn - a cylindrical shaped vessel usually made from heavy glass, a crock material. To churn, a paddle-like stick with a "dasher" was raised and lowered repeatedly until the agitation beat the cream into butter. The butter was skimmed from the milk and put in molds to be shaped into pounds of butter. We drank the fresh buttermilk.

Milk freshly taken from the cow was called "sweet milk." A cousin, currently living in California, related that when living as a child in the city of Little Rock, she visited our farm for the summer. Mother had her churning milk and Cousin asked how the butter and buttermilk was formed. She always thought the sweet milk came from the cow's front two teats, and the buttermilk from the back two teats of the cow's udder. Mother quelled the laughter of bystanders and patiently explained the process to a city child who had no knowledge of farm life. Terminology was unique to the culture; loaf bread purchased from the store was called "light bread."

On the farm, our big meal was the mid-day dinner. This is when farmworkers "came in" to eat and rest. After dinner, some people took a short nap before returning to the fields. My father would lay on the floor under the south window because there was usually a breeze blowing in that window. His neck was so short that his head did not touch the floor, but he always slept soundly. For supper, at the end of the day, we ate dinner leftovers, or many times we crumbled cornbread into the fresh buttermilk, and just ate "bread and milk" for the evening meal.

Before long, it was bedtime, and we washed up in the "foot tub," a circular aluminum container that stood about one and one-half feet tall, and one and one-half feet across. Water from the pump was poured into the foot tub where you washed, "sponged," your body, and immersed your feet in the water to clean your legs and feet. A bath was taken on Saturday nights in a #3 tub. This was the time when you could actually sit in water for a bath. Our family emptied our water after each bath, but in some farm families, several persons bathed in the same water before it was poured out.

The rain barrel was another source of water. This was a barrel that was placed underneath the eaves of the roof to catch water when it rained. We did not drink this water, but it was used to bathe, wash clothes, and for other household uses.

Wash Day was always a lot of work. The washerwoman would put water in the #3 tub, take a washboard or scrub board and a bar of lye soap, and wash the clothes. This was done by putting clothes in the water, lifting a garment onto the washboard, lathering the garment with the soap, and rubbing the garment up and down against the washboard. It was this agitation that cleaned the clothes.

A fire was built under a big round black iron pot. The white clothes were scrubbed, placed in the iron pot to boil, and returned to the scrub board for more agitation. White clothes were then put in a rinse-water into which "bluing" had been poured. When white clothes were scrubbed, boiled in the pot, rinsed in bluing water, and hung on the clothesline, they were the brightest, prettiest things imaginable, blowing in the wind. Ladies took great pride in their white, bright, clean clothes hanging on the line.

Ironing was an art. An iron, made from cast iron, was placed on hot coals that were kept heated in a container. The iron was ready to be used when saliva, applied to the finger, sizzled when quickly touched to the iron. The iron was then applied to clothes which were stretched on an ironing board. As the iron cooled, it was continually placed on the coals to reheat. A thick cloth was placed over the handle of the iron to protect the hand of the person ironing the clothes.

Another difference from today was the outhouse. The outhouse was an experience. Between the hen house and the smokehouse was the path to the outhouse. The outhouse was the equivalent of our modern-day restroom. There were no indoor toilet facilities on the farm during my childhood. One went to a little building, placed a distance from the house because of the smell, where there was a wooden box-like apparatus with a plank to sit on with a round hole cut for the buttocks. The waste dropped to a large hole dug in the ground. It was a scary, smelly, unpleasant, but necessary experience. I sat on that apparatus and was afraid I would fall through the hole. Thank God for today's restroom conveniences.

During the evening and night hours, when it was too dark to go to the outhouse, there was a "slop jar" in each house, where one took care of necessary bodily functions. The slop jar had to be emptied, contents thrown out on the ground away from the house and cleaned each day for use the next night.

Our family was progressive enough to have a concrete floor put in our outhouse, and a toilet tissue holder to replace the traditional newspaper. For toilet paper, Montgomery Ward or Sears and Roebuck catalog sheets of paper were rubbed together to soften and used as toilet paper. In public places, such as schools and churches, the outhouse, also called "privy," had separate facilities for males and females, like today.

As we compare "what was" then, we are thankful for "what is" now.

All neighbors acted as villagers to help raise all children. Every responsible adult served as your parent. They watched us. Reportedly, my great-grandfather was in ill health, and we were told that he was going to die.

Consequently, he began to sell off pieces of the property. He improved and held onto the balance of the acreage. Rev. and Mrs. McKinney bought a lot, as did Mr. and Mrs. Wallace and Henrietta Redd. They, in addition to Mr. Albert Fulford, bought adjoining lots on Tamo Road, which paralleled the railroad tracks. They constantly monitored to make sure we "walk the straight and narrow" to become good productive citizens.

As a child, I remember a sacred area of the farm, where there were two brick pillars through which a path led to a cemetery. In later years, I was told that descendants of Ben Franklin were buried there. Reportedly, approximately 11 graves of these descendants were on the site. In the 1950s and early 2000s, I was able to locate four grave headstones that displayed names of a Ben Franklin Family, Other headstones have apparently been submerged.

II

IDLE HANDS THE DEVIL'S WORKSHOP

Mom and Dad never intended for their children to have idle hands. As soon as we could walk, we had chores to perform in the house. As we became older, we "graduated" to helping Mom in the yard. We helped Mother carry or "tote" water from the pump, to plant the flowers, and the gardens. We milked the cows, "slopped" the hogs, and brought eggs from the hen house, without breaking one egg. The chicken nests were either built around the walls inside the hen house or built outside on stilts above the ground in rows of about six individual nests per row.

Another daily task was to carry drinking water, in a bucket, to the "field hands." These were the workers who labored under the hot sun from sunup to sundown - and from daybreak to dusk dark - chopping or picking cotton.

I loved planting the flowers, climbing the trees, and doing almost every outdoor activity. Mother planted flowers along the front of the porch and the fences on the yards. We had a big lawn area between our house and Marzell Baptist Church, with a "Weeping Willow" tree in the middle of the lawn. The grass was kept beautifully green and cut, and flowers were all along the fences. I remember most vividly the tulips, lilies, marigolds, and zinnias.

Food preservation was everybody's job. Everyone helped with gathering, preserving, and storing the food. We had a huge vegetable garden and "truck patch." Vegetables were picked from the garden and taken "to the house" and washed. Tomatoes were "blanched," and the skin removed, green beans were snapped, and purple hull peas, English peas, lima beans, and butter beans were all shelled. Corn was cut from the cob, okra was trimmed, and all vegetables were cleaned and prepared to be put in jars and canned. The youngest children always had to wash canning jars - thousands of jars! Not one speck of dirt was to be left inside the jar or around the rim at the top. The cleaned and prepared food was put into the quart or pint jars and placed in a "pressure cooker." The jars and food were cooked for a specified time - according to the contents. The cooker must always be allowed to cool down before opening the top. Mother once received a bad burn from steam when she opened the pressure cooker too soon.

A highlight of the canning season was the visit to "Jordan's Orchard" located about four miles south of the Dalton farm. We took "foot tubs," #3 tubs, bushel baskets, and other containers and headed for the orchard to pick peaches, apples, and other fruits. It was a fun time, and we ate as much as we possibly could. There were rows and rows of all kinds of fruit in the orchard. Upon return to the farm, the younger crew washed jars in #3 aluminum tubs while the older, mature youth and adults took pans, carving knives, sat under the big Chinaberry tree in the front yard, and peeled and prepared the fruit for canning. We picked berries, plums, persimmons, apples, and other fruit from bushes and trees on our farm. Nothing was wasted. The peelings, plus any seeds or discarded food, were given to the hogs.

Upon removal from the pressure cooker, the jars were sat on a shelf on the back porch, tables, or elsewhere to cool. They were then taken to the farm's "smokehouse" and stored on the many shelves that were built around the walls of the smokehouse. The building was called the smokehouse because the meat was smoked and hung from the ceilings, in the center of the building to be preserved until cooked.

Meats were produced on the farm. Pork and beef animals were grown specifically to supply homegrown meat for the family. We fed "slop" to the hogs, which consisted of leftover food, scraps, fruit peelings, dishwater, old milk — any kind of old leftover food. Leftovers were put into a big bucket, which sat behind the kitchen stove, and fed to the hogs every morning.

From one to six hogs were killed at a time. I cherish the picture of Grandfather Rodgers and his son, Felton, with six hanging hogs. Neighbors came for "hog killing time"; everybody worked, and everybody took meat home. A hog was chosen and slaughtered, usually by being hit in the head with an axe or shot between the eyes. The hog was then lowered, headfirst, into a big barrel of scalding water, taken out and turned around and the rear end also scalded. The hog was taken from the barrel and put on a table where all the hair was scraped from the hog. The hog was then hung up by the feet, washed good, the head cut off, and the insides removed (intestines, liver). After a thorough washing, the hog was taken down, cut into smaller pieces, and distributed. "Everybody always got some. You always fed the neighbors," said Lenard Taylor, an experienced farmer from Ladd, Arkansas.

Youngsters eagerly awaited the "gutting" of the hog. The pancreas (the melt) was removed, the meat was washed, seasoned with salt and pepper, put on the wire of a "coat hanger," and roasted over fire like a wiener. It was tasty, but not much meat, so the kidneys also were split in half, washed, seasoned, and roasted. "The roasted meat with a slice of "light bread" provided a tasty meal for many hungry individuals," related my nephew Milton Carl Henderson of Tamo.

There were no freezers on the farms, consequently, fresh meat could be stored in the "ice boxes" for only a limited time. A block of ice, purchased from the icehouse, or the Iceman, would only last about two days before it had to be replenished. The icebox was an upright wooden container where blocks of ice were stored on the left, with a storage area for food on the right side. Ice was delivered daily, or every other day, from the icehouse. Sometimes we went to the "icehouse" to purchase blocks of ice, which were handled with large ice tongs.

The meat was canned in jars, just like vegetables and

fruits. Some of the fresh meat was "salted down" for three days, then put in a little house where the meat was smoked with hickory wood, and/or other smoking techniques, for an entire day. Following that procedure, if properly done, the meat was "cured" and would last all year without refrigeration until used. Daddy would just go into the smokehouse and cut down a ham when needed in the kitchen.

The smokehouse was like a store. It contained preserved fruits, vegetables, and meats for consumption. Deep holes were sometimes dug in the ground where sweet potatoes and/or "Irish" (white) potatoes were placed and covered with dirt to keep them from freezing and be edible. Some farmers had a "potato bin" - a small "hut-like" wooden container built slightly off the ground and filled with hay. Potatoes were stored in the hay without touching each other. Other farmers just threw potatoes in a pile in the corner of the cotton house or other place of storage. Every portion of the hog was used. Excessive fat was used to make "lard," a predecessor of today's shortening, for cooking. The hooves and fat of the hog were used, with ashes, to make lye soap for cleaning.

The process for beef animals was the same, but a few milk cows were kept for fresh milk. Beef animals selected to be slaughtered were "put up in the fattening pen," and they were fed corn and water for approximately 30 days. This process was to "clean them out" and create a better flavor in the meat. Instead of scraping off the hair, the process with a hog, beef had to be skinned to remove the hide - or outer covering. The "fattening pen" was a cleaning process used for other animals, as well. Before killing chickens, they were put in a "fattening pen" to be cleaned out and to purify the meat for consumption.

The family always raised *chickens.* Some were "hatched" - a process where the hen sat on her eggs until baby chickens emerged from the fertilized eggs. In addition, every spring, Mother ordered baby chickens from a hatchery. She ordered "yellow buff," Rhode Island red, white rock, and other brands. However, her favorite was the yellow buff chicken. Mother had good luck raising chickens and only lost very few. Also "setting hens" sat on fertilized eggs until baby chicks were hatched. The rooster was king of the chicken yard, with his harem of hens.

The ordered baby chicks, called "biddies," arrived in flat boxes and placed in the chicken house - an approximate 9x10 foot heated house with a trap door that opened to an exercise yard for the baby chicks. The chicks were fed "mash" and small grains from food trays. These were cleaned every day, along with the wood shavings that were placed on the floor of the house for cleanliness. The baby chicks remained there until they grew large enough to roam on the regular yard.

At the adolescent stage, baby chicks were called "pullets" and were large enough to survive on "the yard" on their own. They were also large enough to be prepared for the dinner table. Pullets were fried for tender chicken dinners, and older hens were stewed with dumplings, baked, or otherwise prepared for consumption. Living on the farm, we followed the life cycle of chickens from the hatching from the egg to the dinner table.

The most common ways to kill chickens were to twist their necks or cut off their heads with an axe. After killing the chicken, it was placed in a container of scalding water briefly, removed, and the feathers plucked. After feathers were removed, the chicken was briefly held over a fire to "singe" the fuzz and tiny feathers that could not be plucked. The head and feet were removed, the chicken split, the insides removed, and the chicken cut into pieces, for frying or stewing. Baking chickens were left whole. There was nothing better than a baked hen with cornbread dressing. You were tantalized "for miles" by the aroma. Chicken was also canned, put into jars, and preserved on shelves until consumption, just as the fruits and vegetables.

When the cotton gin was operating, we had a section called "The Mill." The corn that was raised in the fields was grounded and made into a "cornmeal" to cook. Certain corns were used to feed the animals. Consequently, farms were self-contained and produced all of the foods needed for consumption. It was hard work, but everybody was healthy and relatively happy, as this was the only lifestyle to which we were exposed.

Mom and Dad were very active with the Jefferson County Farm Agricultural and Home Demonstration organizations. Our farm was a key site for community training and demonstrations. Mother was very active with the 4-H Club and organized the first group of local farm women to process canned meats in metal containers, preserve fruits and vegetables in jars, and make bed mattresses. I remember my sister Vhaness baking Parker House rolls and canning vegetables to enter into 4-H Club competition. My siblings and I washed so many canning jars that we vowed never to wash another jar when we became adults.

Dinner was served in the back porch diner. The tantalizing aroma of chicken prepared a variety of ways. Fried or boiled corn, peas or beans, greens, fried okra, cornbread, peach cobbler, berry pie, bread pudding, cake, molasses bread, or other foods was torturous as we waited on the back porch to eat. The kitchen was too hot, and the dining room was reserved for Sunday dinner and special occasions. On special occasions, we also had homemade ice cream. Ice cream custard was cooked in the kitchen and cooled on the back porch. The cooled custard was poured into the ice cream bucket. Ice and salt were tightly packed around the bucket in the wooden container, and the cranking began. We took turns turning the crank until it became too hard to turn, and the eating commenced.

Our past time on the back porch while eating was to watch the cars passing on the highway. Every car that passed was, in turn, assigned to one of us on the back porch (e.g., every 2nd car, or every 4th car). Consequently, we always hoped for a good-looking car. When a "rattle trap" vehicle came along, it was cause for loud and boisterous laughter. We also waved at all of the train engineers and the "man in the caboose," as the freight trains lumbered, and passenger trains sped by, on the nearby railroad track.

While we had a great time claiming or disclaiming cars based on their appearance, we were never, ever, permitted to poke fun at the appearance or conditions of people. This would be cause for a good whipping with the switch. We had to go outside and break a switch, or small branch, from a bush or tree. If the switch was not big enough, Mom went out and brought back a bigger one. We were never, ever to think that we were better than anyone else. There was a big wooden container on the back porch, called "the quilt box," with a large door opening to the front. As clothes became too small, or other recyclable materials became available (materials for quilts, etc.) they were washed and stored in this container. Thus, we usually had clothes to share.

When we visited Cousin Juanita, who claimed my mother as a blood sister rather than a cousin by marriage, we took clothes, and she always fed us dinner and loaded us down with vegetables that they grew. Cousin Juanita always prepared the best fresh-picked and cooked purple hulled peas, fried corn, okra, tomatoes, cornbread, peach cobbler, and "all the fixings." Also, we cannot forget the ripe watermelons, that you could always find growing on the vine! The best eating was to bust the watermelon in the watermelon patch and scoop out "the heart." This was the sweetest and best part of the watermelon.

We were always taught respect because every person was our brother or sister and "equal in the sight of God." We were trained to help rather than hurt, to give a "hand up," and to share.

Our family was one of the few families in the community that had electricity and owned a radio. The generator in the cotton gin provided electricity. Neighbors came from miles around to hear the heavyweight champion of the world, Joe Louis, fight. He was the pride and joy of the Negro community. When Joe Louis beat Max Schmeling for the world championship, there was pandemonium!

"No Work, No Eat" was a concept that was drilled into us, every child was taught good work ethics. "You don't work, you don't eat" was instilled at an early age. We planted gardens every spring and harvested enough food in the fall to last throughout the winter. In later years, our family arranged to meet on weekends to plant the gardens and "truck patches" in the spring, cultivate the gardens during the summer, and harvest the crops in the fall. As a child, I ran along behind the mule and the plow, picking up potatoes and other vegetables. In later years, my children briefly followed the tractor to harvest vegetables. The harvested food needed to be of a sufficient supply to last throughout the year. We canned and froze vegetables, fruits, and other commodities needed to feed the family.

Although the families had fun at work, the children vowed to never work in gardens as they grew older. However, as adults, each youngster grew a garden, and son Delano, after retirement from the corporate world, was employed by the University of Minnesota as a master gardener to teach the art of gardening to others.

We also had a legacy that we must work in order to survive. The schools for "Negro" children did not have typewriters, but we had a typewriter at home, and Mother made sure that each of us learned how to type. It is this typing skill learned at home that I have used all of my life. I typed my papers in high school and college and typed term papers, documents, and did secretarial work for others. As I progressed along the career path, typing was the first job that I obtained wherever I relocated.

Mother insisted we learn to do everything - there were no male and female chores. Brother U.G. was taught to drive at age 10, and the girls at age 11. I learned to drive a tractor as well as a truck and car. My brother was a great cook, in fact, he earned money to go to college as a chef in a local Pine Bluff restaurant. He was also a well-known musician, earning money in college as a member of a local orchestra. I remember the placards advertising: *"Chester Guydon Orchestra, featuring U.G. Dalton on Trumpet."* There was a picture of my brother blowing his horn. Their theme song was "Stardust," featuring the trumpet solo. They played engagements as college students, and one wintry, slippery night they were in an accident returning from an engagement. U.G. suffered a broken nose and a few other injuries. He was taken to Links Hospital for Negroes, where he was hospitalized for a few days.

When enrolled at the University of Michigan, U.G. was a member of the marching band. He was inducted into the United States Marines during the Korean War, and in order to travel and perform with the elite Marine Band, he needed a new trumpet. Mother told him to prepare to participate. She was refused a loan at a local entity and borrowed from another city at an inflated price in order to purchase the horn. My parents sent the horn overnight to U.G. He was seen on theater screens across the nation playing with the U.S. Marine Band. An excited neighbor told Mother and, needless to say, the entire family went to the movies. The determination to succeed results from a legacy of achievement.

III

THE LEGACY

Grandfather Dalton was widely acclaimed for his industriousness and ingenuity. William Dalton, the father of Ulysses Grant Dalton Sr. was a slave who cut rails to buy his freedom and then cut rails to buy the freedom of his wife, Emily. They had six children.

Ulysses Grant Dalton, Sr. was born in Mississippi in 1868 to former slave parents William and Emily Dalton. Both parents died when Ulysses Sr. was 17 years of age, and he defrayed the funeral expenses of his parents by cutting and splitting rails. He worked in the cotton fields until he earned sufficient funds to bring him to Arkansas. He came up the Arkansas River by boat and landed at Lake Dick near the towns of Wabbaseka and Altheimer. There he began his career as a farmer and businessman.

Grandfather worked as a field hand, saved money, purchased land, and built a cotton gin about the year 1910. This was a feat almost unheard of for Blacks. I will use the words Blacks, African Americans, Negro, Colored, Nigra, Nigger, whatever was used at that time in history by particular populations. At that time, the word Negro was used by educated individuals, whereas segregationists used words such as Nigra or Nigger.

After developing the farm and business at Lake Dick, grandfather sold those holdings and purchased land at Tamo, Arkansas. There he built a house, a cotton gin, and a general store.

According to Mr. J. H. Robinson, Editor of the Negro Spokesman Newspaper:

> "By hard work, honest toil, and ingenious management he acquired a large farm, on bought and erected one of the first gins to be owned and operated by a Negro in that part the state. … Having successfully operated his farm and gin there from 1901 to 1918, he purchased a large building at Tamo, where he organized the Farmers Gin Co., operating a 3-stand Gullet Gin from 1918 until 1932 when it was destroyed by fire. Undaunted he immediately built another gin structure, equipping it with a later style Pratt outfit. With Professor Tracey, Anderson, Watson, and possible others, he launched the Negro colony organization at Southbend. His career as a businessman is worthy to be emulated by both White and colored. His counsel to his many students of business was: No man can be kept in servitude who is capable thinking he is way to Freedom. His motto was love to all and malice toward none."

U.G. Dalton Sr. married Roberta Crawford and had six children. U.G. Dalton Sr. established a legacy of determination, education, entrepreneurship, and service to mankind - a guiding light for generations to come. He demonstrated an ability to succeed or achieve under hardships and adversities. Thus is the legacy and backdrop of the U.G. Dalton & Sons cotton gin and general store at Tamo, Arkansas.

The Cotton Gin was quite an accomplishment for our family. African Americans had limited access to resources for business ventures. It was through a joint effort *"That W.C. Roundtree, of the one part and U.G. Dalton on the other part, agrees one (1) complete Gin outfit; Viz. 1 Boiler & Engine, 3; one Double Box Hydraulic press, One (1) Steam heater, one (1) Pumo, flues, elevators and other fixtures and connections necessary to make a complete system; and the above-named outfit shall be purchased from the Gullett Gin Vo., Amite, La."*

The United States Food Administration in Washington D.C. wrote a letter dated April 18, 1918, asking Mr. Roundtree to withdraw his application, citing the operation of a gin in Tamo, 1 mile north, and a gin at Grady, 3 miles south. Mr. Roundtree proceeded with the application and the gin was purchased.

On July 11, 1918, Wiley C. Roundtree signed a deed stating that:

"I do hereby grant bargain, sell and convey unto the said U.G. Dalton, and to his heirs and assigns forever, the following:

All machinery, tools, etc., pertaining to the Gin plant bought from the Gullett Gin Company on or about June 22, 1918, and installed on land deeded to the said U.G. Dalton by Mrs. J. A. Roundtree, said land located in Section Twenty-four (24), Township Seven (7) South, Range Seven (7) West. The said U.G. Dalton assumes all obligations to the Gullett Gin Company and all others who might have claims against the said plant."

The debt to Gullett Gin Company was paid off by U.G. Dalton in 1930. Other properties were also purchased from the Roundtree Family. On February 10, 1928, Mrs. Josie Roundtree, a widow, for the sum of $900, deeded *"to U.G. Dalton and his heirs and assigns forever"* the lots that comprised the Town of Dalton, and other properties. Needless to say, my ancestors were progressive.

IV

SOUTHBEND: BLACK HISTORY LOST, STRAYED

According to Mrs. Ruth Teal, of Tarry, Arkansas, four men formed *The Phoenix Development Association, Inc.* They were Mr. U.G. Dalton, Sr., entrepreneur and farmer of Tamo, Arkansas; Professor J.E. Clayton of Chicago, Illinois; Mr. C.H. Tracy, farmer of Tarry, Arkansas, and Dr. J.B. Watson, President of Branch Normal College, later renamed Agricultural, Mechanical, and Normal College (AM&N) College, Pine Bluff, Arkansas. The attorney was Mr. Wiley C. Roundtree. Newspaper accounts stated that:

> *Governor Frank O. Lowden, former governor of Illinois, arranged for the Phoenix Corporation and about 125 families to farm and eventually own 2200 acres of land. Negroes were encouraged to put down money when the crops were harvested. The idea was to make landowners out of sharecroppers.*

Mrs. Teal, daughter of Mr. C.H. Tracy, related that the Corporation also operated a school, complete with a school board. The teachers were Velma Dalton, wife of Chalmers Dalton, and Katy Copeland, sister of Ruth Teal. Mrs. Teal later joined the corporate staff as a bookkeeper. Mr. Curtis Dunn, who lived in Southbend in 1933, and attended school in the fifth grade, says Southbend was called "Nigger Town," because of the number of residents and the level of Black management involved. Mrs. Teal said there were many wholesome activities and people came "from the city" to Southbend to participate in debating, singing, boxing, and other activities.

Subsequent research that I did shows that Southbend eventually consisted of approximately 22,000 acres of land. Mr. Dunn related, "Blacks tried to buy the land. They raised money at church, at school, and everywhere, but the money still had to come through White hands." This research did not show there were accounts of a school system or of the credits earned by students. All had been deleted or lost. Southbend, Arkansas was so named because the Arkansas River flowed south to that point, then curved back north, flowing upstream for some distance, before continuing in a southeastern direction.

Southbend had a noted history centered around an enormous cotton plantation started in 1840 by Dr. John A. Jordan. With slaves bought at the New Orleans, Louisiana auction, he built a stately plantation mansion in 1854 that was built on a 10-foot-high brick foundation, due to the danger of floods. The bricks were made by the slaves from Clay which they dug from the banks of Lake Dian. This mansion, with the use of slave labor, was said to have cost $50,000 at that time. After several ownerships, Governor Lowden bought Southbend and built a large plantation store in 1915, thought to be the largest of its kind in Arkansas. The flood of 1927 destroyed the store, but the mansion survived until 1953 when it was destroyed by fire. Governor Lowden was said to have the finest fishing resorts on Lake Dian and Silverlake that could be found. They were beautiful and served as resort areas for affluent visitors.

Mrs. Teal continued with her history of the struggle of Black ownership of Southbend. Mrs. Teal said, *"We leased the land for four years. Whites made it hard. We borrowed money from Holthoff, big ginners at Gould, Arkansas. Although they paid the loan monthly. we were charged interest for the entire year - we were overcharged. When I questioned how there could be such a large interest balance at the end of the year, I was told by Daddy to be quiet. We borrowed money from Holthoff, and we sold the cotton to Holthoff. Mr. Fish was the Bookkeeper for Holthoff, and I was Head Teacher at Star City. Mr. Fish was on the school board at Star City and when I questioned mistakes in the bookkeeping for Southbend, I was thrown out of a job."*

The occurrence of Blacks always owing White landowners, and never being able to pay off their debts, was a common theme, mostly due to "bookkeeping errors." According to Mrs. Teal, a number of things contributed to the demise of Southbend; the flood of 1927, the detrimental effect on the farmland, *"didn't get crops in on time, extravagant purchases, and flaws in management."*

I remember visiting and spending the night with my grandparents when they lived in the Southbend mansion, along with Mr. and Mrs. Tracy. Uncle Chalmers and Aunt

Velma lived in a smaller house nearby. Uncle Chalmers Dalton and Mrs. Ruth Teal were store clerks and managed the plantation store. However, the only historical account of the time that Blacks managed Southbend was two sentences that appear in the Lincoln County archives; *"after the flood of 1927, Lowden leased the land to others, until his death on March 20, 1943. The property was controlled by a Board of Directors until 1950."*

Mrs. Ruth Teal was one of the most educated females in Arkansas, having received her Bachelor's degree from Bishop College in 1924, and her Master's degree from the University of Arkansas at Fayetteville in 1952. She recalls that in 1939 they could stay no longer at Southbend. However, because she had a teaching contract for another year at Southbend she had to remain and was made to move from the top floor of the mansion to the basement, the former slave quarters.

Mrs. Teal stated that Mr. Tracy had been involved in a successful venture in Louisiana and it was thought that could be implemented in Arkansas. However, success was not to be at that time. A newspaper article states that in the 1950s, the plantation was auctioned off in small tracks, with one successful bidder being of African American descent, Mr. Memphis Johnson. This researcher's visit to Mr. James Johnson, the grandson of the named purchaser, revealed that this never occurred. Mr. Memphis Johnson was told to bid on the land, and he would be provided the money. This did not happen, consequently, the managerial history of Blacks at Southbend, Arkansas, was lost and strayed.

Some of the prominent farmers in the area were Messrs. C.H. Tracy, Willie Pridgeon, J.P. Morgan, Watt Winston, Roy Collins, Henry Towns. Also, prominent farmers included Messrs. Fuller, and Snead, and Toy Grice, father of noted photographer, Geleve Grice. There were numerous Blacks who owned land that was located on Highway 65, between Pine Bluff and Grady. However, in later years, and in today's economy, it is rare to find Black landowners and farmers, with large holdings, located on the highway. Even most of the small farms, which are not owned by African Americans, have been swallowed up by larger corporations.

Many city residents lost revenue with the loss of Black farmers and small farms. Trucks had pickup points in the cities to bring cotton choppers and cotton pickers from the city to the farm to plant and harvest the crops. Choppers and pickers worked "by the day," and cotton pickers could make from $1.50 to sometimes $5.00 per 100 pounds, depending on how much the farm owner would pay and how much cotton the picker could pick.

The farmers, workers, and families worked hard during the week, and on Sundays, we went to church. Sunday afternoons, many times, we played baseball or softball. Friends came from all around to play baseball in the pasture that was located across the road from our store. The men played series of ballgames while the women provided snacks, including homemade ice cream, and cheered.

Even today, Black farmers receive inequitable treatment. Mr. Johnson has two sons farming the family holdings, and although they pay their loans off each year, it is still difficult to obtain a bank loan in time to plant the crops in a timely manner. Excuses are given to deny Blacks equitable treatment. In fact, a number of legal suits have been filed against governmental entities relative to the inequitable treatment.

A personal experience is when I intervened on behalf of the farmer who was renting our farmland. When Mr. Maxie Thomas applied for funds, he was denied a loan in spite of the fact that he had paid off the loan for the previous year and had good credit. While living in California, I wrote and enlisted the aid of my California Congressman, Mr. George Brown, who wrote Arkansas Congressman Beryl Anthony, and the Federal Farmers Home Administration (FHA) on my behalf. December 31, 1990, I wrote Mr. Max Roland of the FHA Star City, Arkansas stating that Mr. Thomas had never been late meeting his obligations, had made his payment to the First State Bank of Gould in a timely manner, however, some procedural mistake had been made and he could not access his funds. Consequently, he was unable to pay rent. *"Since the crop from our land was successful, funds have been released by your agency, and previous personal experiences with the FHA have been handled professionally and efficiently, I am requesting an inquiry into the status of the aforementioned funds that have been earmarked for payment of rental obligations."*

I wrote Congressmen, FHA personnel, bank personnel, and everyone I thought could intervene and "do the right thing." Unfortunately, to this day inequitable treatment still exists toward the Black farmer.

Much of the Southbend information was obtained from Mrs. Ruth Teal, and Mr. Wayne Boren, a historian at Star City, Arkansas, the county seat of Lincoln County.

Black farmers lost their land through various activities. Sometimes absentee property owners did not pay their taxes and the land was forfeited, and sometimes land was lost through boundary disputes. For as long as I can remember, we have had disputed differences with adjacent White landowners who encroached on our boundary lines. We have always had to fight, including court battles, to defend our property. Whether "on the highway" or "the lake property," neighbors took more and more rows of our land. Encroachers also thought that with the death of each senior family member the property may be available, whether my father, mother, or brother. They soon found, however, that the property, with the legacy, was cherished by other members of the family. The land would never be for sale or available to be taken. Too much "blood, sweat, and tears" had gone into obtaining and retaining this property ownership. Following Mother's lead, I wrote letters to pertinent individuals explaining our intent, and my sister Velma and nephew Milton Carl had a 6-foot ditch dug on the lake-side property to establish a permanent property boundary to define a line that kept moving in favor of the adjacent landholder. We were willing to retain this land "by any means necessary" to legally continue the legacy.

Often Blacks have been, and are still perceived as non-enterprising, when too often, their ownership and heritage has been stolen, as in "Lost, Stolen and Strayed."

V

THE DALTONS OF TAMO, 1909-1930

Speech by Velma Dalton Gilbert, February 2000

I was very pleased when my friend and relative, Mrs. Goldie Bush, asked me to participate in this program because for the last 12 years my family has been involved with the "Persistence of the Spirit" movement, which resulted in the formation of "300 Years of Black History in Arkansas."

This exhibit is always showing in the Fine Arts Gallery of the University of Arkansas at Pine Bluff (UAPB), even though other showings are in existence. My brother, Dr. U.G. Dalton III, and I were asked by Mr. Henri Linton, Chairman of the Arts Department at UAPB, and a representative from the Humanities Department in Little Rock, to meet at Mrs. Lillian Mazique Johnson's house to contact persons in Jefferson County about notable Black persons in this area. This was the beginning of the search for information. From there the committees were formed and expanded.

Our family, "the Daltons of Tamo," is involved in this history at the University. You see, my grandfather, Ulysses Grant Dalton, Sr., built a cotton gin and a store in Jefferson County in 1918. I cannot at this time talk about the gin without including the store, because they go hand in hand. It was difficult at this time for Black men to secure the necessary licenses and credentials to have a "GIN."

I first must tell you the location of our farm at Tamo, Arkansas. We are located 20 miles south of Pine Bluff, and our farm was sandwiched in between two (2) gins already in operation and owned by Whites. One was at Grady (3 miles south of us, and the other was at Tamo - one mile north of us.

My grandfather was very persuasive and could convince you to go across a railroad track when a train was coming. He was definitely a businessman, and politician also. He made a GOOD FRIEND OUT OF THE COUNTY JUDGE and bought property from him. Grandfather also secured the services of the judge to get the licenses, etc., for this venture.

We still have, in our possession, the contract that was exchanged during the sale of licenses for $1.00. The cost of the gin was $10,000 with $7,000 down, and the balance *of $3,500 to be paid at a later date. Grandfather was charged $500 interest.*

There were numerous Blacks around us who owned their own farms, and the business was evident. The store was known as the "Community Hub" because so many things were done during the fall and spring. The GIN, during off-season, was used to make cornmeal - they would grind the corn from which you had removed the "shucks," the "husks," and the "silk." The store was used as a gathering place for community projects, some of which were conducted by the 4-H Club County Farm Agents, who taught the farmers how to "can" meats and vegetables and grow better crops. Farmers would grow their vegetables, hogs, and cattle, but did not have the expertise to preserve meat to sustain them during the winter months.

Along with owning the gin and store in the community, you had to "furnish" the farmers with survival resources with whom you did business until they could harvest their crops. My grandfather did all of this.

Naturally, there was opposition from the other owners of gins because we were seen as a threat - so much so that orders were issued by one of the gin owners to burn down *our home, and the first effort was made. My mother told us about the paralyzing fear they had trying to keep the store, our house, and the church, which was adjacent to our property, from burning down. We were successful in finding out who the individual was, and how much he was paid, to commit this crime. He was paid $200 by one of our competitors, at Grady, to do the job. There were also two attempts to rebuild, but after the last attempt, my grandfather chose not to rebuild again.*

I have on display a "card" which is a picture of the Gin and Store. Also, on display at the University of Arkansas, is a tobacco cutter, cheese cutter, and other items related to the gin and farm. These items, along with my grandfather's attaché case, are part of "300 Years of Black History in Arkansas" on exhibit at the University of Arkansas at Pine Bluff.

I do not have all of the history of "Gins" in Arkansas which were owned and operated by Blacks in Jefferson County, but I do know that we did have a large group of Black farmers who traded with us, and we were the only Blacks in Jefferson County to be operating a gin at that time.

I feel it serves a good purpose to have these things told to the younger generation and share the multitude of handicaps our forefathers endured in order to survive and prosper.

My grandfather's parents were slaves. Grandfather left Mississippi and went to stay with his sister in Memphis, Tennessee at the age of 15. He had no formal education. I am just wondering today what he could and would do with all of the advantages that we now have - especially with his talents.

The speech faxed to Mildred Dalton Henry on
February 26, 2000.

Cotton was king in our area. Farmers came from miles around in horse-drawn wagons and Model-T Ford trucks filled with cotton to be "ginned." Upon arrival, the wagons and trucks were driven to the back of the Dalton General Store and onto scales to be weighed. The scales were a moveable device built over an oblong rectangular hole in the ground. As vehicles were driven off, the scales would rock to-and-fro. Children gleefully jumped on the scales to see how long we could continue the motion and keep the scales moving.

The wagons were driven around to the cotton gin where large adjustable suction tube-like devices pulled the cotton into the gin to separate the cotton lint from the seed. The fluffy cotton was formed into "bales" and taken to Pine Bluff to be sold and shipped out by trucks. The seed was sold to the Planters Cotton Seed Oil Company to be made into oil and other food products. When cotton was brought to the gin, and there was an insufficient amount to form into a bale, the cotton was stored in the "cotton house" until more arrived. We loved to jump and play in the soft cotton - never considering any danger of asphyxiation or disease. It was just great fun!

Cotton was hand-picked by individuals of all ages. The strap of a cotton sack was draped across the neck and shoulders, and a sack, made with heavy cotton material, was pulled between the rows of the field. The picked cotton was placed into the sack by the handful. Sacks came in all sizes - from short sacks for little children to long sacks that could hold well over 100 pounds. Everyone worked in the cotton field.

When the sack became too heavy, the picker took the cotton to be weighed and returned with an empty sack. Sometimes sacks were left at the end of the row, exchanged, and the picker continued picking to conserve time. At the end of the day, usually "at sundown," all cotton was weighed, and the pickers were paid according to the number of pounds they had picked that day, e.g., $.65 to $1.50 per 100 pounds of cotton.

Cotton choppers and pickers dressed in long sleeve shirts and layers of clothing. Instead of being hot, as onlookers imagined, the extra clothes gave added protection from the hot sun and actually kept the wearer cooler. My four children were sent to the field to pick cotton. After a few hours, the four had collectively picked 12 pounds and knew this was not a career in which they wanted to engage, creating an added resolve to get an education.

Picking cotton was "backbreaking" work. The continual bending to extract the cotton, sometimes from picking two rows at the same time, was tiring. Consequently, some pickers frequently wore knee pads and crawled between the rows. The process of pushing the fingers into the sharp-edged cotton bolls to extract the cotton was hard on the cuticles, tearing them and severely scratching the fingers.

This was the livelihood of farmers, consequently, everyone who was old enough to "go to the field" was expected to harvest the crop. Negro (hereinafter referred to as Black) "sharecroppers," or families who lived on farms owned by others, were all expected to pick the cotton. Many times, marriages were arranged for convenience. On our farm, Mr. Bannister was married to "Sister Baby" - who was two or three times his junior. From this marriage, five children were born who worked on the farm. In rural areas, children were delivered by a midwife who came to the home, used the woodburning stoves to boil water, and used hot towels to welcome the newest addition to the family.

Cotton picking season was from approximately September to November. Consequently, the area schools for Black children remained closed during that time, and children could not begin attending the segregated school until early November. Mother had a 1923 teaching certificate for a term of five months. Likewise, in the spring, oftentimes schools for Black children were closed early in the season so that children could go to the fields and "chop the cotton." This was the process whereby a long-handled hoe was used to remove grass from around and between the cotton plants which were growing on long, long rows in the cotton field. A group of choppers would begin at the end of the rows and move through the field together because they talked, laughed, and sang as they each took a row. When younger, slower choppers "fell behind" the older, more experienced choppers would "catch them up" to the group. When Daddy was not plowing with the tractor, he helped me to "catch up," because I was always left behind.

As the youngest child, however, I was mostly "the water girl." I carried water in a bucket to the field for everyone to drink. There was only one dipper in the bucket, and all drank from that same dipper. If one did not drink the full dipper of water, the water was cast onto the plants. However, each drinker tried to only take as much water from the bucket as they would drink, because it was a long trek to bring water from the pump to the workers. Water was drawn from a well into which a pump had been installed. One first had to "prime" the pump by pouring a little water in the top and quickly pushing and pulling the handle up and down until water flowed from the mouth of the pump. The bucket was then pumped full of water. Pumps were located in several places on the farm as this was the main source of water. A pump was usually placed near the house, and "pump water" could always be found on a shelf on the back porch. There the water was stored until used in the kitchen or for other household use.

Often one had to step over and between barbed wire fences to carry the water bucket because the pump was in a farmyard that also contained animals. Our pump was approximately ½ block from the store, and one block from the Canal that ran behind our house. To this day, I have a visible scar on my left leg from an injury sustained on a fence. After pumping water into the bucket, I was crossing between two strands of a barbed-wire fence and ripped my leg open on a barb on the lower strand of wire. One had to very carefully negotiate those fences and could only carry a bucket or relatively small amount of water at one time. This amount of water was insufficient to combat a burning inferno started by an arsonist.

VI

THE INFERNO

My scared, small, wide-eyed face was pressed against the window as I watched the neighborhood men furiously fight the fire that threatened to consume our store and house. Having previously been attacked by arsonists, our armed guards stationed around the property were vigilant. However, on a windy night, Marzell Baptist Church, next door, was set on fire so that the wind could blow embers over and set our store ablaze. The calculation worked, the church burned, our store burned, and the cotton gin was again destroyed. The bucket brigade firefighters, along with my mom, bravely fought the fire and were successful in saving our home. I cannot imagine the hard work and bravery of the men fighting the blaze with such limited resources.

The arsonist was successful and this time we were unable to rebuild the gin and store. Arsonists caused us to be "red-lined" and identified as an insurance risk. Because of two previous arson fires, there were guards stationed around the perimeter of the property. Mother wore a whistle around her neck to periodically check with guards to see if they were awake and alert. This time, however, on a windy night, the culprit torched the nearby church. The arsonist was caught and confessed that he was hired by a gin owner at Grady, Arkansas to burn us out. He was sentenced and some individuals say he served about two months. However, my Cousin Henry said, "That peckerwood didn't serve a day in jail." The arsonist reported that Joe Gocia of Grady, a farm and gin owner, paid the arsonist to burn the Dalton farm. Grady was located three miles south of Tamo, a slice of Arkansas flatland running Southeast along the Arkansas River from Little Rock through Pine Bluff through the tiny community of Tamo, in the southeastern corner of Jefferson County.

This dastardly act placed an additional burden on local residents. They had previously come to our store in horse and wagon for food and sustaining resources. Now they had to travel many additional miles to obtain survival items. Many farmers needed loans, or charge accounts, to obtain resources until their crops were harvested in the fall. This was one of the reasonable services provided by Grandfather and family at the Dalton store and gin.

Saturdays were big shopping days and people could be seen walking and "hitching a ride to town." Whoever was lucky enough to have an automobile would transport others for a small fee, or even pick up a neighbor at no cost. At this time, it was safe to pick up people who were hitchhiking on the side of the road. There was absolutely no fear of anyone getting hurt; in fact, it was the neighborly thing to do. The Union Station on Fourth and State Street was a place where people congregated. Not only was it a meeting place to secure rides to and from the rural areas, the union station, and the bus terminal were the only places in town where Blacks could use public restrooms.

Saturday nights were party nights. Our farm is located one mile south of Tamo, and on Saturday nights the owner of the Tamo General Store sat the jukebox outside, locked up the store, and went home. People partied well into the night. I listened longingly from my bedroom window to the loud music and seemingly good time floating on the airways across the mile. We were not allowed to go to Tamo or Grady, located 3 miles south of the farm, to participate in the party festivities. Some schools were also used as social centers. My cousin, Augusta Berry, was an excellent pianist. With a drink and a piano, Augusta would "tickle the piano keys" for numerous weekend dances and social activities at Oak Ridge school and elsewhere. Some musicians on tour also visited the school.

VII

JIM CROW AND SEGREGATION

Segregation was very demeaning and destructive to self-esteem. According to excerpts from *Racial Etiquette: The Racial Customs and Rules of Racial Behavior in Jim Crow America, 1906*,

> *Most southern White Americans who grew up prior to 1954 expected Black Americans to conduct themselves according to well-understood rituals of behavior. This racial etiquette governed the actions, manners, attitudes, and words of all Black people when in the presence of Whites. To violate this racial etiquette placed one's very life, and the lives of one's family, at risk.*

> *Black men were called by their first names or were referred to as "boy," "Uncle," and "Old Man" - regardless of their age. Black women were addressed as "Auntie" or "girl." Under no circumstances would the title "Miss," or "Mrs." be applied.*

> *This practice of addressing Blacks by words that denoted disrespect or inferiority reduced the Black person to a non-person, especially in newspaper accounts. In reporting incidents*

involving Blacks, the press usually adopted the gender-neutral term "Negro." For example. An accident report might read like this: "Rescuers discovered that two women, three men, four children, and five Negroes were killed by the explosion."

The rules of racial etiquette required Blacks to be agreeable and non-challenging, even when the White person was mistaken about something. Under no circumstances could a Black person assume an air of equality with Whites. Black men were expected to remove their caps and hats when talking with a White person. Those Whites, moreover, who associated with Blacks in a too friendly or casual manner ran the risk of being called a "nigger lover."

Blacks and Whites were not expected to eat together in public. In some places, it was okay for Blacks to enter a restaurant to buy food to take out or to stand at the end of a lunch counter until their order was taken. Usually, they would then leave and wait outside for their food to be brought to them. Nor were Black customers always allowed to use store implements such as plates or dishes or even boxes. Black customers commonly brought their own tin pails and buckets to be filled.

The White owners of clothing stores did not allow Blacks to try on clothing as a general rule, fearing that White customers would not buy clothes worn by African Americans. In most towns, Black customers knew which stores could be expected to treat them with respect while not breaking the rules of racial etiquette.

Many public places, parks, and entertainment centers excluded Blacks altogether after 1890, frequently by law if not by custom. In some communities Blacks could attend public performances but only by using separate entrances in the back or via an alley. In public halls, theatres, and movie houses, they always sat upstairs in the so-called "nigger heaven" or "buzzard roost."

Law rather than custom separated the races in public transportation. Some towns and municipalities put Blacks in the rear of the streetcars [or buses] while others required them [to be] up front where they could be watched by the car's operator. Custom did not allow motormen or conductors to assist Black women with bags or parcels. In general, it was expected that Blacks would give up their seats to White passengers during peak or crowded times.

Some towns required separate entrances to public buildings. White clerks in stores and ticket stands always served White customers first, although no state or municipal law required this practice.

The color line and the codes of racial etiquette were also strictly observed in public hospitals, with separate wards [or hospitals] for Whites and Blacks. A similar Jim Crow code of conduct applied even in the U.S. Army. It was not until Eleanor Roosevelt intervened in WWII that Black nurses were allowed to care for White soldiers, even though a serious shortage of nurses existed. The Black nurses were used prior to Roosevelt's intervention to attend to German prisoners of war rather than U.S. soldiers.

The whole intent of Jim Crow etiquette boiled down to one simple rule: Blacks must demonstrate their inferiority to Whites by actions, words, and manners. Laws supported this racist code of behavior - or whenever racial customs started to weaken or break down in practice - as they did during the Reconstruction Era. When the laws were weakly or slowly applied, Whites resorted to violence against Blacks to reinforce the customs and standards of behavior. Indeed, Whites commonly justified lynching and

> *horrible murders of Blacks during the Jim*
> *Crow Era as defensive actions taken in*
> *response to Black violations of the color line*
> *and rules of racial etiquette.*

Jim Crowism was experienced by all of my family. In Pine Bluff, there was one movie house for Blacks - the Vester Theater. In the other two theaters, the Saenger and Strand theaters, Whites sat on the first floor, and Blacks sat in the balcony. Whites entered the front through a lobby, to padded seats on the first floor. Blacks entered a side door, paid at the window, and immediately went up a flight of stairs to wooden seats in the balcony.

One day, a White neighbor told Mother that she saw my brother, U.G. Dalton III, on the movie screen at the Saenger Theater. Of course, the entire family went to the balcony of the Saenger Theater to see this family member serving his country and marching with the United States Marine Corps Marching Band. When my brother U.G. was attending the University of Michigan, and drafted into the U.S. Marines, he needed a new trumpet to be in the band. My parents provided the trumpet, and there he was, proudly marching for all of the world to see.

The world, however, was not aware of the self-esteem assaults that we endured. Many days, our family members walked downtown or walked the three miles from our house to AM&N College rather than ride the bus and suffer the indignity of being asked to get up and give our seat to a White passenger. This person may enter the bus and singularly occupy a seat designed for three persons. Blacks had to stand although two empty seats were available. A sign posted in front of the bus stated: "Whites seat from the front. Colored seat from the rear." The two empty seats could have been occupied.

"My Cup Runneth Over" became a prevalent feeling of protest. The local Kress 5 & 10 Cent Store, located on the corner of Main and Fourth Streets, was greatly supported by Black shoppers whose money was solicited but whose presence was demeaned. For instance, Mother made statements like, "It's mighty funny that we can spend our money to purchase goods, but we cannot sit down and eat food and drink like other people." There was a lunch counter that did not provide service to "Colored People." At the back door, there was a water fountain for "Whites Only" on the East wall and another for "Coloreds" on the West wall. This was enforced no matter how much money the shopper possessed, making it clear that the money was welcomed but not the individual. These demeaning circumstances were observed by children as they watched the indignities inflicted on their parents, who only wanted to provide treats and happiness for their children.

With the advent of the civil rights movement and the bravery and mistreatment of the Little Rock Nine, unrest swept the land. My sister, Vhaness, relates how my mother, sister, and other community residents determined that "enough was enough." Meetings were attended, and strategies planned, and sit-ins were initiated in Pine Bluff to desegregate the lunch counter facilities. Participants were instructed to be courteous, orderly, well dressed, and show up in force to sit at the lunch counters. There were specific speakers, such as Attorney Wiley Branton, and Attorney George Howard who were the spokesmen to the newspapers, radio, and other news media. Pine Bluff Attorneys Branton and Howard stood shoulder to shoulder with Attorney Thurgood Marshall (later appointed to the U.S. Supreme Court) in the fight for the Little Rock Nine to integrate Central High School in Little Rock.

When AM&N College President John Watson insisted that titles be used for his staff and called for a student boycott of a racist and abusive merchant, his life was threatened. His leadership was supported by the Black community who then initiated a community-wide boycott of the Marx Brothers store. The enlightened leadership at the college had a profound impact on the community and the nation at large.

The lunch counter in Kress 5 & 10 Cent Store in Pine Bluff, Arkansas was desegregated as were other lunch counters. My sister, Vhaness Dalton Henderson, relating the events to me in Oak Hills California, in 2011, stated, "Kids, grown folks, everybody participated - were in the streets. You would not have had it if you had not fought for it." Anger still radiated in her voice as she spoke of the events, even after all of that time.

Attorney Wiley Branton, who advocated for the Little Rock Nine, later went to Washington, D.C., and became a nationally known civil rights attorney. Attorney George Howard, whose daughter was personally involved in the Little Rock Nine Central High School movement, was subsequently appointed a federal judge by President William (Bill) Clinton. Attorney Wiley Branton's brother, Leo, became a noted attorney in Los Angeles, California, successfully defending famous personalities such as Angela Davis, Nat King Cole, Jimi Hendricks, Dorothy Dandridge, and Miles Davis.

It is said that "birds of a feather flock together." Paul Branton, who descended from a family of entrepreneurs and lawyers, was a good friend of my brother, U.G. Dalton III, who descended from a family of entrepreneurs and educators. Both played trumpet and were participants in various events and organizations. The Branton Family owned the 98 Taxicab Company in Pine Bluff which was heavily patronized by Black clientele. On rare occasions when we needed a taxi, we always called a 98 taxicab to be transported. In fact, taxicabs who catered to White clientele did not transport "Negroes." Segregation permeated the land.

Protest and refusal to accept inequitable treatment is nothing new for the family. My Aunt, Odessa Dalton, relates how the grandmother on her dad's side had a strong Native American background, with high cheekbones and reddish skin. "She was washing greens to cook for dinner and an ole White man let his horse drink out of her bucket. She cursed that man and he cursed her. She picked up a hoe and chased that man and his horse all around. I don't know what tribe she was from, but that peckerwood got away from there." Odessa Mae Dalton was 93 years old when interviewed in Pine Bluff on January 1, 1986.

Another incident of "I won't take it anymore" was told by Cousin Henry Strickland. In 1934, while plowing the cotton field, "some White man" mistreated Henry's mule. When Henry protested, he was called a Black Son-of-a-Bitch (SOB). Henry called the man a White SOB and hit him. Henry had to immediately leave home and the area because, as expected, a White posse came to his house to get him. Henry related this incident during an interview in Little Rock Arkansas 2009, and said, "those were some rough days child." Blacks having to flee their homes was not uncommon. Noted Photographer, Geleva Grice, relates in his book, A Photographer of Note:

> "We moved from Tamo in 1935. My father and uncle Willie Richardson got in trouble with the White rider named Price. He worked for a big farmer named Joe Gocher, I couldn't say how it's failed. He's not down here had a big place down by Grady, owned thousands of acres of land, hundreds and hundreds of mules. Price was his rider like an overseer. Anyway, he and my father and uncle got into it - they cut up a little bit. They brought them up to Pine Bluff and put them in jail. Years later I did a picture of Price, at some reunion, a graduation down in Moscow. I'm sure, he

didn't have any idea who I was - the man who got put in jail and run out of the county for beating him up. My father left a big farm down there, but that's the story of how we got out. Back in those days, it was kind of tough, you know. We wanted to get out of there because we didn't want any problems. We fled in disorder! My uncle left too, with his wife and child, came up to Little Rock with us."

There was good reason to fear for one's life. In March 1866, approximately 24 African American men, women, and children were lynched just outside of Pine Bluff, according to a letter from Wayne William Mallet to U.S. Senator Thaddeus Stevens. If this eye-witness account of men, women, and children hanging from trees is accurate, this was the largest mass lynching in the United States, exceeding the 1891 lynching in New Orleans. According to the *New York Times* on February 15, 1892, two Black men – Culberth Harris and John Kelly - were lynched in front of the Jefferson County Courthouse as 5,000 to 10,000 spectators watched. The area also has the dubious title of the most lynchings of any county in Arkansas.

Ku Klux Klan

Following the Civil War, White terrorist groups, consisting largely of disgruntled Confederate veterans, sprang up throughout the South.

"Reconstruction eventually produced a wave of anti-African American sentiment. White organizations such as the Ku Klux Klan, which aimed at intimidating African Americans and preventing them from taking their place in society, sprang up throughout the North and the South. ... By the late nineteenth and early twentieth century, lynching had become a weapon used by Whites against African Americans throughout the country. Between 1882 and 1990, approximately 1,750 African Americans were lynched in the United States. Victims included women who had been accused of a variety of 'offenses' ranging from testifying in court against a White man to failing to use the word "mister" when addressing a White person."
<u>Reference Library of Black America, Vol. II. P. 376</u>.

Black Wall Street

Historians are finally acknowledging the 1921 horrific burning and assault on the thriving Greenwood Business District, referred to as Black Wall Street, in Tulsa, Oklahoma. The massacre of hundreds of African Americans by White racist mobs occurred over unfounded rumors of the assault of a White female by a young Black male. The thriving Greenwood community had an assortment of Black businesses, including two banks, hotels, and other self-sustaining neighborhood enterprises. The unfounded assault charges were later dropped but the damage had been done. Reportedly 35 square blocks were burned, bombed, and destroyed, and approximately 600 Black businesses were reduced to 21.

Historical accounts report that in Greenwood, the home of approximately 10,000 African Americans, hundreds were killed, and more than 1,800 were left homeless over the 18 hours of violence. Blacks were even blamed for the so-called "riots," and some were indicted or sent to internment camps. The destruction of Black Wall Street is one more murderous, sadistic incident of mob violence against African Americans in America, "the land of the free and the home of the brave."

Despite the mistreatment, African Americans have served valiantly to protect this country. For instance, 40,000 African Americans served in the Union Army during the Civil War. Before that time, in the 1866's the 10th Cavalry Regiment of the U.S. Army, nicknamed "Buffalo Soldiers by American Indians tribes, was a regiment that served on the western frontier, and in peacetime and wartime. Before that time, in the 1700s, Crispus Attucks, a Black man, was the first to die during the Revolutionary War in our fight for freedom against England. During World War II, the famed Tuskegee Airman flew fighter planes and bombers. They were requested to be protective escorts on numerous fighter missions because of their unprecedented success.

It must be remembered, however, that for all of the dastardly acts of the Ku Klux Klan and hate groups, there were always some Whites performing great acts of kindness. For instance, Judge Wiley Roundtree, who purchased the cotton gin with my grandfather, in 1918, deeded the gin and all holdings to Grandfather and *"unto his heirs and assigns forever,"* for the sum of one dollar. The document states:

> *"The plant was purchased by W.C. Roundtree and U.G. Dalton by a joint order to the Gullett company, it being their intention to operate it as the Farmers Gin and Supply Company of Tamo, Arkansas., and W.C. Roundtree later being drafted into the Army is unable to carry his part of the obligation and U.G. Dalton is to carry both the interest Roundtree was to have had with his own interest."*

Attorney Roundtree was also the legal authority and helper for the Southbend venture. The Dalton Gin, including steam engines, boilers, heaters, smokestack, motors, generators, the cotton house, everything associated with the cotton gin, was insured by Continental Gin Company, Birmingham, Alabama, for $3,300. The Dalton cotton gin, general store, and holdings became an integral part of the Pine Bluff and Jefferson County culture.

Tamo On the Map

The little community of Tamo produced numerous achievers. One such individual was Mr. Ira K. Wells, born at Tamo on July 1, 1898, to William and Emma Brown Wells. Ira attended Professor Samuel Vaster School at Tamo and attended high school at Branch Normal in Pine Bluff. He received a Bachelor's degree at Lincoln University in Pennsylvania, a Master's from the University of Pittsburgh, an honorary doctorate from Lincoln University, and an honorary Doctor of Laws degree from Allen University. He organized the Negro Democratic Executive Committee, and in 1932, Ira was one of the country's leaders who helped change the majority of Black American voters from the Republican Party to the Democrats. In 1944, he founded and published Color Magazine, the first Black American pictorial magazine. It was patterned after Life Magazine and reached a circulation of over 100,000 before its demise 14 years later.

Mr. Wells' sister, Genoa Wells Keith, and husband Solomon Keith, Sr. were close friends of my mom and dad. Solomon Keith, Jr., was a childhood and lifelong friend of my brother, U.G. III. They were dressed up in "knicker" pants and spent the night at each other's homes. During the summer months, "Little Sol" went north to work with his uncle on the Color Magazine. The Wells Family, and other noted achievers, attended Professor Samuel Vaster Elementary School at Tamo. In later years, both my mother, Mrs. Alma Rodgers Dalton, and my sister, Mrs. Vhaness Dalton Henderson, taught at Vaster School.

The fertile soils produced many other gifted well-known artists who had deep roots in the Tamo area. Famous musician, Miles Davis related in his autobiography that the influence on his music was derived from country churches near Noble Lake, three miles north of Tamo. While walking home from church with his grandparents, the blues rhythm of the gospel music permeated his creative blood and imagination. He wrote music that tried to capture that feeling. I was baptized in the waters of Noble Lake, so the area holds a very special place in my heart.

VIII

THE PINE BLUFF RENAISSANCE

Pine Bluff, the county seat of Jefferson County, was a cultural and intellectual center for Arkansas African Americans who made great achievements, in spite of profound adversity. Likened to the Harlem Renaissance, there was an intellectual and cultural innovation among African Americans in music, literature, theater, the arts, medicine, business, and politics.

The area produced African Americans who achieved milestones in career fields including education, medicine, literature, the military, music, and other professions. Pine Bluff was the center of Black influence which produced critical back leadership. African Americans from across the state converged in Pine Bluff to the college and to the Colored State Fair, owned by Wiley Jones, which brought an estimated 20,000 Blacks together annually. According to the *Arkansas Delta: Land of Paradox*, at the beginning of the 20th century, African Americans owned four barbershops, 19 grocery stores, four butcher shops, three shoe shops, four blacksmith shops, five saloons, 12 restaurants, two hotels, and the Delta's first Black-owned bank.

Enterprise and Blacks could flourish in Pine Bluff around 1889. Wiley Jones, a former slave became a barber; invested in real estate; owned a Pine Bluff trolley car company; a horse racing track; real estate holdings, including a resort; as well as several other business ventures. The richest Black man in Arkansas, Wiley Jones was worth $250,000 at his death which equates to about 2 ½ million dollars in today's economy. Many prominent statesmen and performers were drawn to the culture in Pine Bluff. These included but were not limited to, Dr. Martin Luther King, Dr. Mary McLeod Bethune; and internationally known artists such as Isaac Hathaway, Duke Ellington, Clark Terry, and Eldridge Cleaver, Mohammed Ali, and Jackie Robinson.

The "Chitlin' Circuit" was a performance venue for Black entertainers during segregation. Famous Black blues and popular music celebrities that came through Pine Bluff's Chitlin' Circuit included Ethel Waters, Charlie Parker, Louis Jordan, Cab Calloway, Muddy Waters, B. B. King, Louis Armstrong, Howlin' Wolf, The Staple Singers, Ike and Tina Turner; and James Brown, Johnny Taylor, Little Milton, Bobby Blue Bland, Z.Z. Hill, Johnny Taylor, and many, many others. Many of their hit songs were also written by AM&N graduates.

Religious singers on the Chitlin' Circuit, often performing in Pine Bluff school gyms and churches, were The Five Blind Boys of Mississippi, The Pilgrim Travelers, Mighty Clouds of Joy, The Loving Sisters, Sam Cooke, Walter Hawkins and the Hawkins Family, Andre Crouch, Cleophus Robinson, Shirley Caesar, The Gospel Keynotes, The Clark Sisters, and many others. Pine Bluff was a cultural Mecca.

Many doctors, lawyers, educators, and progressive citizens practiced their professions in Pine Bluff at the turn of the century. According to *The Illustrated Industrial Souvenir of Pine Bluff and Jefferson County, 1906*, there were numerous Black businessmen from our area.

Practitioners of Medicine were extremely proficient and included Dr. G. W. Bell, who graduated from Dartmouth College in 1894. Born a slave, he specialized in chronic diseases of women and children. He was elected by "a board of White trustees" to be President of Southland College, and later a State Senator of the State of Arkansas' Fifth District, *"where he established a commendable reputation among the prominent legislators of the state."* A reputed *"careful and painstaking physician,"* Dr. Bell built an infirmary and hospital, *"where his numerous patients were taken to receive careful attention."* Dr. George A. Flippin, who graduated from the University of Illinois College of Physicians and Surgeons in 1900, *"with a specialty of surgery and diseases of women and children, built up a large and lucrative practice."*

Dr. H. L. Jordan graduated from Meharry College where his *"bright intellect won him the highest honor of being chosen valedictorian of his class, and he also won the first prize in surgery."* Dr. J. W. Rowland, a graduate of Meharry Medical College in Nashville, Tennessee had a successful practice in Pine Bluff. *"He is Secretary of the United States Board of Examining Surgeons, which position he fills with honor and credit."*

<u>Dr. S.M. Miller</u> owned and operated a hotel, café, drugstore, and laboratory.

"His hotel is the best equipped in the South for the accommodation of Colored guests. Dr. Miller has not only made himself famous as a specialist in treating all chronic diseases of man, women, and children, his new discovery of famous non-poisonous mixtures as remedies has made him a great reputation. He manufactures various mixtures for all the ailments of suffering humanity, especially females, and can furnish hundreds of testimonials of his marvelous cures for both White and Colored. He does an extensive mail-order business, and his mixtures are sent all over America. Dr. Miller's laboratory is a model that is an index to his high scientific development and his untiring efforts and research along the line all undiscovered mysteries."

<u>Dr. J.W. Parker</u>, the dentist for my family, graduated from Northwestern University of Chicago. He was also a prominent member of St. John African Methodist Episcopal (AME) Church. Most of the medical offices were located in the Southern Mercantile Building on 4th and Main Street.

The drugstore on the corner of State and Fourth Street was operated by the Jones Family and was next door to the 98 Taxicab Company, on State Street, owned and operated by the Branton Family. The Southern Mercantile Building on Main Street and the Masonic Temple Building on State Street were managed by African Americans and were professional centers for Black businesses. The Masonic Temple was hailed as the finest structure in Arkansas outside of Little Rock.

Educators and Professionals were drawn to the growing advancement of Pine Bluff as a commercial and educational center. Professor Marion R. Perry, located to Pine Bluff in 1886, was named Principal of the Colored High School and was made Superintendent of Colored schools. His administration of our public schools was a highwater mark of Negro education in Pine Bluff. Professor William Townsend was the third principal of the high school in Pine Bluff, succeeding Professor Perry and Professor Thomas McMakin. Coming to Pine Bluff in 1893, Professor Townsend was appointed Principal of Greenville School in 1894 and later unanimously elected to the position of Principal of Missouri Street High School, later to become Merrill High School. "*The Pine Bluff public schools were open for the reception of Colored pupils in the public hospital of 1869, and since that time the schools have had a nine-month session with few exceptions. The Colored people of Pine Bluff have always enjoyed educational advantages superior to those of most other towns in the state, and the schools have always kept pace with the best educational methods,*" according to *The Illustrated Industrial Souvenir of Pine Bluff and Jefferson County, 1906.*

There were equally prominent and qualified members of the Jefferson County Bar Association, such as attorneys <u>A.L. Burnett</u>, <u>J. F. Jones</u>, and <u>S. C. Pryce</u>, a former slave.

The <u>Windham Brother's Construction Company,</u> *"The most enterprising and most successful firm of Colored contractors in the State of Arkansas"* was located in the Southern Mercantile Building. They built some of the most modern office buildings and private residences in Pine Bluff, Arkansas, Monroe, Louisiana, Columbus, Ohio, and other communities across the nation.

On January 10, 1905, <u>Mr. James Jones</u> began the reputation of being *"the oldest continuous whiskey man in the county"* when he assumed management of Wiley Jones and said to have *"catered to the wants of the public who desire fresh beverages"* and quality cigars.

> *"Among the oldest and most popular resorts in Pine Bluff is the prominent thirst-quenching establishment at 223 Main St., which was owned and operated by the late Wiley Jones, and who enjoyed an extensive acquaintance and a reputation as a good judge of fine whiskey, as well as fine horses."* Operated by Wiley Jones Brothers, in 1905, *"This house enjoys an extensive trade in retail business and does also the largest business in the jug line of any house in the state."*

<u>Jake Mosby</u> operated *"one of the deservedly popular resorts in Pine Bluff. And patrons can rest assured of getting the best liquors on the market. Another important consideration is that the conditions maintained by him are of an order that is calculated to promote pleasure and entertainment, they are being an entire absence of that class of people who destroy the pleasure of others by their own noisy and boisterous conduct."*

<u>Offie Lites Studio and Adams Photography</u> preceded Geleve Grice for prominent photography studios in the community. Located in the Southern Mercantile building, Mr. Grice was the official photographer for AM&N College and the University of Arkansas in Pine Bluff. At homecoming games, Grice could be seen roaming the football field taking pictures of interest. The photograph depicted in this book shows Mildred Dalton Henry, Louise Slack Dalton, and Velma Dalton Gilbert. Ladies were expected to be well-dressed at homecoming games and were considered improperly dressed if wearing casual clothes.

In addition to businesses located in the Black-owned Southern Mercantile Building and Masonic Temple buildings, many Black-owned businesses were located in other buildings along Main Street. These trailblazers blazed the path for generations to follow.

<u>Educational ICON Branch Normal College</u> was one of two leading educational institutions in Arkansas. It contributed

largely to the growing advancement of Pine Bluff as a commercial and educational center.

> *"The Branch Normal College is a branch of the University of Arkansas and was originally established in Pine Bluff as authorized by the act of the General Assembly of the State of Arkansas in 1873. The sole purpose of this institution is to educate the Colored youth to a degree of standing alone in the world and of bettering society in general.*
>
> *The main college building is an extensive structure of about 16 rooms, a two-story brick, and thoroughly equipped with the most modern conveniences and nothing is lacking in the course that is taught here…. Besides a brick building utilized in teaching the literary branches, and the modern brick structure for the medical department, a large conveniently equipped double-storied, brick dormitory is used."*

My parent's generation attended Branch Normal College, which was later changed to Agricultural, Mechanical, and Normal College, which finally changed to The University of Arkansas at Pine Bluff. Mother always advocated, "Keep your own money," an idea that permeated in the progressive Black community. Within a few blocks of Agricultural, Mechanical, and Normal College (AM&N) on Cedar Street in Pine Bluff were a variety of Black-owned businesses. There were restaurants, cleaners, barber shops, shoe repair shops, grocery stores, service stations, a new and used furniture store, and a liquor store. A few blocks further was Yancy, a furniture and refurbishing store, and two funeral homes: Perry's Funeral Home, for whom Mother wrote insurance, and Miller's Funeral Home.

In the 1940-1950s, some medical professionals, such as Dr. C.A. Lawlah, our family general practitioner, and Dr. J.W. Parker, our dentist, were located in the historic Southern Mercantile Temple, on the corner of 4th and Main Street. Adams Photography was another predecessor of Geleva Grice photography. Another occupant, Attorney George Howard, Sr., a prominent attorney in the Little Rock Nine desegregation case, and later appointed a federal judge by President Bill Clinton, was the Dalton Family attorney. Later Dr. Hyman, Gynecologist, and Dr. Harold Flowers had medical offices in the Masonic Temple building on 4th and State Street. The Masonic Temple housed other professionals and Black-owned businesses.

It is significant that the "hub" of the Black community was located near "The College," because most of the business owners attended or were associated with the Historically Black Agricultural, Mechanical, and Normal College (AM&N). This regional state-operated college was formed traditionally to educate Negroes and prepare "lesser advantaged" and economically advantaged students for entrepreneurship, good work ethics, competitiveness, and success. Because of disadvantaged backgrounds in the South, the college accepted almost all applicants.

AM&N graduates who became nationally and internationally renowned are too numerous to name. Native Pine Bluffians earned a Ph.D. degree from Columbia University, Harvard University, and other prestigious institutions. They also led the protest movements for civil rights at the local and national levels, were pilots and leaders in the military, ambassadors to foreign countries, and served under several U.S. Presidents.

It is noteworthy to mention the wealth of Blacks at the turn of the 20th century. In this environment, in spite of a thriving Black business community, there was a record number of lynchings in the area. There were Grammy Award winners and noted Black artists participating in the "chitlin' circuit." They performed valiant military service, and the Tuskegee Airmen from the area were celebrated. There was a powerful presence of the Black church. African American Pine Bluff area natives served in all areas of American society, and it was in this environment of expected achievement that the Dalton Family was prominent.

IX

TOWN HOUSE EDUCATION

The town house that we envision today was not exactly what my parents were able to secure in Pine Bluff. It was an older house, badly in need of repairs, and inhabited by rats that took a while to exterminate. The house that Mother was able to obtain, in the right location, had leaks in the roof and other unacceptable conditions. She wanted a new house, however, unable to secure a loan, Mother would not entertain defeat. She obtained a loan to rehabilitate the old building and demolished the walls to the bare floor. She constructed our home from the floor up. The lady was ingenious! The joke among my siblings was that no matter how late we came in from an affair, Mother would get out of bed and come to us with her house plans in hand. She persisted until the house was built!

Mom was always a fighter. She took the lead in writing various legal entities about the farm inequities and about the business. Mom was a leader in disputed affairs and Dad was the supporter. During that segregated environment, the matriarch had much more freedom than the patriarch. There were many times Mom placed her hands on her hips while addressing a dispute. If a male had taken such a posture, he may be considered an "uppity nigger" and may be lynched. Too often some

Black men were perceived as weak, however, that was a survival technique for many.

The house, strategically located on the west side of town at 121 North Oak Street, was converted into a four-bedroom and bath home, with a living room, dining room, kitchen, complete with a front and back porch. St. John African Methodist Episcopal (AME) Church was two blocks to the north, the First Missionary Baptist Church was two blocks to the south, and the St. Andrews Episcopal Church was at the corner.

The bus line was one and one-half blocks away, and two grocery stores were within two blocks. Merrill High School was three blocks away, and AM&N College was within three miles, a walking distance. We were on the "paved" side of town with an alley separating our house from our White neighbor and several others. A row of hedges bordered our property, but the neighbors could see over them. One day the neighbor infuriated Mother by saying that we "looked like decent people!" This neighbor would never, ever have the education that my mother had obtained. However, this was the superiority-inferiority Jim Crow mentality and environment that some people wanted to maintain. We were business and property owners and knew the importance of pride and dignity.

Homeownership has always been a key cultural variable in the Rodgers and Dalton Family Legacy. It was my job to cut the grass and hedges and maintain the yard. I loved it and the property was well kept. Across the street in front of us, facing Barraque Street, were the owners of

Robinson Mortuary for Whites and other large 2-story houses with maids. Some of those remaining neighborhood houses are on the National Registry of Historic Houses. Mother always maintained that her children would get an education and never have to work as a maid, or "in White folk's kitchens."

Our backyard was adjacent to two sisters, Miss Nora and Miss Sarah Jones, of the prominent Wiley Jones Family. Wiley Jones was a leading businessman in the community. One of his endeavors was to establish and own the transit system - a mule-drawn streetcar line in Pine Bluff. The streetcar and Mr. Jones are currently depicted in Pine Bluff on a building mural entitled "Main Street" - how the street looked in 1888. Mr. Jones also owned a racetrack. The sisters lived next door to, and were long-time members of, St. Andrews Episcopal Church - nicknamed "The blue vein church." Reportedly, one's blue veins had to be discernable in order to join the church, however, this was definitely not the case by the time we moved into the neighborhood.

My parents, especially my mother, always reached out for the betterment of others. Our Pine Bluff home had a little shotgun house behind it, which housed an elderly couple, Mr. and Mrs. Meyers, and their granddaughter, Essie. Mrs. Meyers stayed home, sometimes cooked for outsiders, and Mr. Meyer cut grass and mowed lawns for a living. Essie said her husband was in the service and asked our parents, who she called Mother and Dad, if she could stay with us. Daddy stayed on the farm most of the time, so they agreed. Essie was quite attractive, did not finish high school, and "lived in the fast lane." She usually brought and shared Bar-B-Q dinners when she came home late at night, and always insisted that we study hard, get a good education, and "do what you are supposed to do, not as I do." Essie put a value on education, loved to dance, wore expensive clothes with beautiful high-heeled shoes, and was a big sister that insisted we stay in school and "walk the straight and narrow." Those were exciting times as we hurried out of bed to eat the delicious late-night feast.

There was a row of "shotgun houses" in the next block on Pullen Street. The houses were named so because they were usually built with three or four rooms straight back, and if the front and back doors were opened, one could shoot straight through the house without hitting a thing. As we walked to and from school each day, there was usually someone sitting on the front porch of each of the six to eight houses in the block. We had to speak to each person or be labeled "uppity" - a label that required discipline. We developed quite a speaking repertoire.

Every member of the community was an overseer of youth behavior. Any one of the adults felt empowered to correct any observed misbehavior - even to the point of applying a switch to correct the behavior. This was followed with a subsequent report to the parent. If this happened, another switch or board of education was applied to our seat of learning. The unofficial School Board of Education was every adult in the community.

Elders were to be respected, and we were constantly reminded to "stay in a child's place." Parents and community residents attended school activities, and everybody knew every family and what child belonged to what family.

When Mom and Dad bought a house in Pine Bluff, at 121 North Oak Street, my grandmother, Mama Roxie, stayed with the children for a period. Mother was teaching at Tamo, and Dad was operating the farm at Tamo. The children were enrolled in the Pine Bluff Schools to receive a nine-month education. Roxie Mabry married Henry Rodgers years after the death of my mother's mother, Lillie Hambrey. One of my chores as a child was to wash the dishes, and I always broke dishes, although repeatedly warned by Mama Roxie. One day she went to the canal and brought back a long switch. I thought it was a tree. When she finished whipping me, I did the impossible; I stopped breaking dishes. At that time, it was called discipline and "train a child in the way he should go," not child abuse.

Seeking a formal education was not negotiable. "To be or not to be" - there was no question. There was never a question of *whether* one would go to school but rather *where* so that arrangements could be made. We had a legacy on which to build.

Mother's cousin, Juanita Jones Howard, told me that my mother "left footprints that could be seen in the dark." Mother's education did not come easy. She began teaching with a ninth-grade education because, at the time, she was the most educated in the local community. She attended a school that was operated by Mr. Martin Pleasant, which was also attended by Mom's brother, Felton, and neighbors Aus, Bertha, and Lucy Berry. There was a culture of achievement expected. In the photo of U.G. Dalton's 1924 automobile, of the friends seated in the car and on the running board; most became teachers or entrepreneurs.

Mother entered college in 1939 and finished in 1953. She went to school every summer until 1953, when she graduated college with my sister, Velma. Each summer, a group of teachers attended AM&N College in Pine Bluff in order to expand their educational qualifications. These included my Aunt Velma Ramsour, Mrs. A.B. Wynn, Ms. Johnny Johnson, and her sister, Ms. Mamie Johnson, all of whom took summer classes to earn college credit.

During the war years, specifically 1942, Mom accepted a typist position at the Pine Bluff Arsenal. She could have been promoted to higher positions, if she accepted other shifts, however, she was explicit in saying that she must be home when her children came from school, at approximately 3:30 P.M. Blacks were hired at the Pine Bluff Arsenal as a result of the manpower shortage during World War II. Black women, particularly, benefitted from the new job opportunities created by directives from President Roosevelt's Fair Employment Practices Committee.

Mom worked at several schools, such as the two-room schoolhouse with Mrs. Morris on Princeton Pike in Jefferson County; Oak Ridge two-room schoolhouse at Moscow with Mrs. Blackburn, teaching for $50 per month; and Tamo Elementary School with Professor Vaster and Ms. Mamie Johnson. In the Pine Bluff area, she worked at Main Street Elementary School, where she taught in 1943. Ironically, in 2007, I met one of Mother's Pine Bluff Main Street Elementary School first-grade students at St. Paul African Methodist Episcopal (AME) Church in San Bernardino, California.

Mom signed a contract in the Watson Chapel School District in 1946, witnessed by Nathaniel Richmond, where she worked at the Jefferson County Training School. The name later changed to Coleman Elementary School, in honor of a Black principal. Mother worked at Coleman for eight years. Many years later, I was employed as the first Middle School Counselor in that same school and district. Mom also taught at Grapevine School in Grant County in 1953. In the Grapevine District, she taught at St. Paul School from 1957 to 1961. Mother was a progressive, determined worker, always seeking opportunities for the betterment of the family. She taught school wherever she relocated.

My father died in 1958, and when Mom remarried and moved to St. Louis, Missouri, she worked in the Kinloch and Wellston School Districts from 1962 to 1971. Mother took the Arkansas Department of Education tests and received a teaching certificate in 1952, graduated AM&N

College with a Bachelor's degree in 1953 and had a teaching certificate issued by the State of Missouri in 1961. The real estate agent's remarks that *"you don't need no house 'cause your little nigger kids ain't never gonna 'mount to nothing nohow"* were constant motivators. Of the four children of Alma and U.G. Dalton, Jr., all four children finished college, three earned Master's degrees, and two earned Ph.D.'s, the highest educational degree.

The legacy endures through the generations. The quality of education for generational family members was also a factor as shown by the schools from which we matriculated. These included Cornell University, MIT, University of Michigan, University of Minnesota, Wayne State University, Washington University, the University of Arkansas at Fayetteville and Pine Bluff, Southern Illinois University, Texas Southern University, Texas Woman's University; Tuskegee Institute, and the University of Missouri. The graduates became veterinarians, chiropractors, lawyers, teachers, counselors, physical therapists, artists, administrators, and entered other professional careers.

I have fond memories of the two-room schoolhouse with a black pot-bellied wood stove that I attended early in childhood. Mother was one of two teachers at Oak Ridge, along with Ms. Susie Blackburn, who served as principal at Oak Ridge Elementary School in Moscow, Arkansas. Mother received her teaching license in 1923. Teachers had to build the fires to heat the schoolhouse, cook the meals for the children to eat, provide social services, and teach academics. Teachers insisted that students learn and do their schoolwork. Hands were spanked with a ruler if students did not bring their homework assignments completed, and students were paddled if they misbehaved. It was not considered child abuse. Parents were solidly behind the teachers discipline, and teachers were well respected in the community.

My mother's 1923 contract was with the Jefferson County School District 17 "for the term of five months, at a sum of $50 fifty dollars for each school month." Her "Arkansas Teachers License 1924" was signed by N.P. Keith County Superintendent and her "Teachers Contract 1925" was signed by S.W. Blankenship. In conversations with grandsons Ronald and Donald Blankenship, the twins related how their grandfather, Samuel Wirt Blankenship "was the only school board member of District 17 that believed that African American children should have an education. He prevailed, and there were schools for all children." Historically Black Colleges (HBC) made higher education available and affordable.

Mom and Dad sent all four children to AM&N College in Pine Bluff, Arkansas. Many times, when it was time for registration, money was not available. Mother insisted we go register on time, tell the college officials to let us register, and she would bring the money. We did, they did, and she did. This could only have happened for us at a Historically Black College (HBC). The schools were small enough for officials to know each student and family. As youths, we were unaware of these nuances, but progressive families were known for determination, achievements, and keeping their word. "A man's word is his bond" was instilled at an early age. Also, most officials at the Historically Black Colleges were from similar backgrounds and knew the struggles experienced to survive and achieve in the segregated environment.

My brother finished AM&N College in 1950, majored in music, and 13 years later, in 1963, was the College Band Director. Sister Velma, and my mother, Alma Dalton, finished in 1953. I was a college dropout, entering college in 1949, dropping out in 1951, and returning in 1969 to finish in 1971 with a Bachelor of Science degree in Music Education. During the interim period, there was marriage, relocation to St. Paul, Minnesota, five children, a divorce, and a return to Pine Bluff, Arkansas. I re-entered college at 38 years of age, a divorcee with four children to support. Sister Vhaness, also a college dropout, finished years later with a Bachelor of Science degree in Elementary Education and was an elementary school teacher for more than 35 years in the Pine Bluff, Arkansas, and St. Louis, Missouri area school districts before sickness forced her retirement.

During the war years, college for Mother was interrupted as she accepted a clerical job at the Pine Bluff Arsenal. However, she continued her educational pursuit and teaching. Mother graduated college with her daughter Velma in 1953, 30 years from the time she received her teaching license and began teaching. She was one of many employed teachers who attended college in the summer. Aunt Velma Ramsour Dalton, who married Uncle Chalmers, came to Pine Bluff from Dermott, Arkansas every summer to stay with us and attend college. Aunt Velma was a jovial, excellent pianist who made the best banana pudding in the whole world!

Daddy was also a role model for education. He was sent from the farm at Tamo to Little Rock, Arkansas, the State Capital, to study accounting. Dad was groomed to be the bookkeeper for the store and business manager for the farm. Although he was qualified, he would not be hired in non-Black-owned businesses in that segregated society. Other family members were also entrepreneurs and made necessary living arrangements to maintain and pursue business enterprises. Dad and Mom remained at Tamo when Grandfather, Uncle Chalmers and Aunt Velma, and others went to Southbend, Arkansas to establish the Southbend Colony where we farmed 10,000 acres of land on the Southbend Plantation.

Mom and Cousin Juanita were more like sisters than cousins. Cousin Juanita's remark that my mother "left footsteps that could be seen in the dark" was a road map published with sweat and hard work, and we were expected to follow the map.

Arts education was automatically part of our training. We memorized and recited a poem for every holiday and every occasion, without question. Many poems came from the 1932 edition of _Bowles Book of Poems_, which contained poems and readings for every occasion. Mother played piano and directed church choirs for as long as I can remember. Church choirs also sang with "shaped notes" and is where I learned to sing Do-Re-Me syllables, as heard in the movie, "The Sound of Music."

Everyone in our family learned to play an instrument. All the children learned to play piano and then ventured out to other instruments. In fact, my father and his brothers traveled to music conventions singing as an acapella quartet harmony. Mother and Father met at a music convention, where she was also singing with her sisters. The youngest Dalton brother, Chalmers, had perfect pitch and tuned pianos, violins, and most string and brass instruments. I always participated in choirs in high school and college, and in church. It was exciting to sing George Handel's *"The Messiah"* in 1950, in the first presentation of what became a tradition at AM&N College in Pine Bluff, Arkansas. My brother, U.G. Dalton III was a music professor for 32 years at AM&N College in Arkansas and Alcorn State University in Lorman, Mississippi.

Many individuals who were not acquainted with southern customs and culture made derogatory remarks. When I arrived in Minnesota, a colleague remarked, derogatorily, to me, "I have never been south of the Mason-Dixon line, to which I replied, "and you have missed one half of your life because this is where culture for Black folks really exists." In the South, we were enrolled in clubs that taught us how to behave, how to properly set tables and adequately serve, and other social graces. There were always ladies teaching younger populations about academics and culture and how to become productive citizens. When I returned to Pine Bluff, I enrolled my daughters in a "social and literary arts club."

Inter-District Education was prevalent. No complaints were heard, or legal suits initiated when students attended school in a district in which they did not live. It was the normal practice to attend school "in town" to get a better education. This was the option when schools for Black children were closed for children to chop or pick cotton. My parents decided that a five-month education was insufficient and that the educational deficiency would accumulate over the years.

Our Cousin Flossie Dalton, while being raised by my parents, was sent from Tamo to Pine Bluff to attend Merrill High School. Flossie lived with Ms. Myrtle Jones, who was a teacher at Merrill High School, and an educational icon in the community. After completing Merrill High School, "Uncle U.G. and Aunt Alma" sent Flossie to beauty school in Memphis, Tennessee. Upon completion of her studies, they established a beauty shop in a section of the General Store at Tamo for her entrepreneurial venture.

Brother U.G. Dalton III and sister Vhaness were also sent to live with Ms. Jones for a while. After much discussion and soul-searching, our parents decided to buy a house "in town" since all of the children needed a nine-month education. They first tried having people stay with us. Our step-grandmother, Mama Roxie, who married my mother's father, Henry Rodgers, following the death of Grandmother Lillie, stayed with us for a while. Our youthfulness and exuberant activities proved to be too much stress for her. Before leaving, however, Mama Roxie taught me a lesson in discipline. I had a habit of breaking glassware when I washed the dishes after dinner. After repeated warnings, Mama Roxie walked a block to the river, broke a switch off a willow tree, returned home, and applied the punishment designed to break the habit. Anyone ever whipped with a willow knows how it bends and clings. I broke the habit of breaking dishes.

Following Mama Roxie's tenure, on two different occasions, two married couples stayed with the children. However, it was ultimately decided that for the best interest of the children, and family, for Mother to live in town with the children on weekdays, and Daddy remained on the farm. We went to the farm on weekends and spent summers on the farm. Mother obtained teaching jobs in the Pine Bluff suburbs. This was the sacrifice our parents made in order to provide their children with a nine-month competitive education.

It should be known that the nine-month education provided calendar equity for Black populations, however, the facilities, curriculum, and resources provided for Black children were never comparable to that provided to White children. Our teachers, however, were qualified, professional, well-dressed, active in the community, and well respected by students, parents, and the community-at-large. They were our role models.

Teachers told us that when the old worn books from the White schools were sent across town to the Negro schools, it was more important to learn the contents rather than concentrate on the condition of the book. We never received new books. Our teachers, however, were determined to instill self-respect, high self-concepts, and ideals, and prepare us for a world that espoused equality "With liberty and justice for all" but did not practice that doctrine.

Miss Myrtle Jones, my Civics teacher, never married and lived in a beautiful two-story Victorian-style house, complete with Romeo and Juliet type towers. As a child, I envisioned a water-well in the kitchen and a Hansel and Gretel-type oven. Actually, it was one of two houses in Pine Bluff that had a basement, with water in the basement. Located one block from our home, we passed Ms. Jones' house each day going to and from school. It was a landmark.

Unfortunately, this beautiful home fell prey to so-called progress with the construction of the freeway. Other lesser-historical houses, not owned by Blacks, were placed on the National Historic Register. No Black-owned homes in Pine Bluff were placed on this prestigious list, although they deserved to be honored as such. My sister, Velma, also owned such a historic structure.

Merrill High School was *the* high school to which students came from all over Southeast Arkansas to become academic scholars and community leaders. Named after White Philanthropist, Joseph Merrill, who donated money for Black education; Merrill High School was respected throughout Arkansas because of its outstanding graduates and its educational leadership.

Merrill excelled with its competitive choirs and bands, and in sports. In 1933 and 1934, Coach Henry Foster, Sr. led the Merrill High School Tigers football team to win the Black High School *National* Championship. Because of Merrill's close relationship with Arkansas AM&N College, students were constantly exposed to African American trailblazers who came to the campus to speak. The trailblazers included but were not limited to, Joe Louis, Dr. Mary MacLeod Bethune, Jesse Owens, Marian Anderson, and many other famous African Americans.

The Alma Mater was sung with pride and gusto. Just as in the movie "Lean on Me," we had a good choir and competitive music department. My siblings and I sang in the choir, and my brother played trumpet in the band. Mrs. Marjorie Kirby, the choir pianist from whom I took private piano lessons, was also my high school math teacher. In later years she also gave my daughter, Alvia, private piano lessons. We joke about how Mrs. Kirby could be "miles away" and hear you make a mistake.

Merrill High School and other Historically Black schools with limited resources graduated great contributors to society. In 2018, Merrill Alums rejoiced with schoolmate Raye Jean Montague, U.S. Navy Engineer, who designed the first computer-generated draft of a U.S. Naval ship. Other engineers had been unable to do so. She was also the first Program Manager of Ships in the U.S. Navy. Raye Jean graduated from AM&N College when that Black institution had no engineering program. In 2021, another "first" who graduated from Historically Black AM&N College is Pamela A. Smith, the first Black Female Chief of the U.S. Park Service, who was the first in the 230-year history of the Park Service to be appointed to that position. The NBC newscaster said Pamela was from "a little town in Arkansas named Pine Bluff."

Just like with milk from the cow, the cream rises to the top. Leaders also rise to the top. Attending segregated schools provided more opportunities to assume leadership positions. Merrill High School was the premier regional public high school and academically included students came from all surrounding rural areas to attend. Consequently, the academic scholarship was a friendly competitive endeavor. There were several very active families who were known for achievers. A friendly academic classmate competitor of mine was Thomas (Tom) Stevens, whose immaculately dressed mother was my Social Studies teacher. Tom later became President of Los Angeles Technical Trade College in Los Angeles, California. Tom established a contact for me when I came to California.

My brother Ulysses and Eddie Mays were academic competitors. Both obtained doctorates. Eddie received a medical degree and became a dentist in Northern California. Ulysses obtained a Doctor of Philosophy degree and became a college professor. Dr. Eddie Mays' brother, Dr. James Mays, a renowned heart specialist, resided in California. All of the children of Ms. Edna Mays, a single parent were professionals. Then there was the Daniels Family. Mrs. Daniels was PTA President, and all of the children became professionals - especially in education. Arkansas State Representative Henry Wilkins III, to whom I appealed for help in later years, was a classmate of mine. Harold O'Neal, our student body president, was from a family of high achievers, and the list goes on and on.

My peers looked forward to going to school. We achieved, had fun, and were disciplined. A ruler to the hand or paddling was expected if one did not complete the academic assignments. Paddling was a sure bet if one misbehaved. In fact, some previous students do not have fond memories of those days. It is felt that many teachers were more disciplinarians than teachers, that they truly believed in the little song that we sang, *"Reading and writing and 'rithmetic all to the tune of a hickory stick...."* However, we learned.

Speaking in California with a 90-year-old graduate, Mr. Sterling Branton, whose family owned the 98 Taxicab Company, he unbelievably named the Pine Bluff streets, in all directions, in rapid succession. He also vividly recalled, and I, too, could visualize, a blank United States map, and named the states and capitals – again in rapid succession. Drafted into the Army and leaving Pine Bluff at approximately 18 years of age, it still angers Mr. Branton, who now resides in California, that African Americans could not use the public library and did not have access to free books. Even the public bus did not go out to the college, turning approximately 1 mile short of the campus. Mr. Branton is thankful, however, that his grandfather had a large house, with a very extensive library.

We played a game on the Merrill playground called "the whip." Students joined hands and ran with the leader, at some point, curving the line. This caused stress on the last person in line and the goal was to remain standing as the whip was executed. Because of the danger of injury, we were forbidden to play the game. We did so, and one day, players in the middle of the line turned loose, and this caused special stress on a girl in the middle. Dorothy Ann Davis fell and broke her leg. All players were scared to death because the principal, Mr. R.N. Chaney, had a paddle in his office for which he was known. If one could not learn through one end, the head, the "board of education" was applied "to the seat of learning" at the other end. As expected, Mr. Chanay certainly applied the discipline. An academically astute student, Dorothy Ann later became Pastor of Faith Presbyterian Church, the place where I married one of the previous pastors, Rev. Hayward Henry, my second husband.

Merrill High was a large u-shaped two-story building, with a large auditorium and balcony built at a right angle. The building housed elementary and middle students on the first floor and secondary grades on the second floor. When I graduated from Ms. Myrtle Jones' seventh-grade Civics class on the first floor to Mr. Palmer's Math class just above on the second floor, I thought I had arrived! Eventually, a second separate facility was built for the elementary school.

Most of our teachers were also leaders in the local churches. Mrs. Stevens, my Social Studies teacher, Miss Jones, and others were also my Sunday School teachers at some point. Mrs. "Lady" O'Bryant, whose husband, Dr. William O'Bryant, owned the West End Drugstore, taught me to read the little Bible cards as children sat around a circular table in St. John AME Church. Merrill High School Principal, Mr. Chanay, and family were also active members. I grew up in St. John under the tutelage of area doctors, i.e., Dr. C.A. Lawlah and Dentist J.W. Parker; lawyers; business owners; and other professionals. Every adult was your parent.

Lift Every Voice was always a civil rights slogan. Black History was taught to us in school, and we stood and learned every word of "The Negro National Anthem," now titled "Lift Every Voice and Sing," which was part of our "Reading, Writing and Arithmetic" regimen. This song, by brothers James Weldon and Rosamond Johnson, is historically known to build self-esteem and was sung at every school assembly, either at the beginning of assembly following "The Star-Spangled Banner," or we sang "The Star-Spangled Banner" at the beginning of assembly and "The Negro National Anthem" at the end.

There are still those individuals who do not understand and respect the song. We were from a background of abuse of a people from the shores of Africa. We were brought across the graveyard ocean, to the shores of America, to be enslaved, and continued to experience inhuman treatment. However, we survived, and although "Stony the road we trod," we were encouraged by singing, "Let us march on 'till victory is won!"

The Negro National Anthem, also called "Lift Every Voice and Sing," was never intended to replace "The Star-Spangled Banner." It was the outgrowth of the actual experiences of our forefathers, and the song gave hope "out of a gloomy past." It is prayerful with the words: "God of our weary years, God of our silent tears." I think of the movie Glory, and the silent tears of the soldier being unfairly whipped. "Till now we stand at last where the bright gleam of our bright star is cast." The song is uplifting! I get "chills" and experience so much pride, each time I sing the song. I can relate it to my history and that of my forefathers. I will forever stand for the singing of that song.

The historic Merrill High School building that served Black students from 1886 to 1976, was torched by arsonists on July 7, 1986. All but the auditorium of the large brick building at West Pullen and North Linden Streets "crashed into flaming rubble at about midnight," according to the Pine Bluff Commercial Newspaper. In September 1986, I visited Pine Bluff and was devastated to see the fire had destroyed the beloved Merrill High School. I was shedding tears when another woman walked up who had attended Merrill. She said, "I knew by the way you were standing there that you went to school at Merrill." The lady was also visiting from California, was a former classmate, Doretha McCoy Webster. A few years later it was her husband, John Webster, who went to Sacramento, California to incorporate my nonprofit, community-based organization when I moved to San Bernardino. I had been heavily involved in the Merrill Restoration Alliance before moving out of state, and I was appalled at the sight.

X

THE CHURCH THAT BINDS

The church has always been a cornerstone of the Dalton and Rodgers families. Mother took piano lessons and played for numerous churches, schools, and community events. Dad was the Superintendent of the Sunday School at Shiloh AME Church for as long as I can remember. U.G. Dalton Sr. was known throughout the region as a statesman and established the church at Tamo, was an adviser on business affairs for the district, and was an ordained minister. He also established St. Stephens AME Church at Pastoria, Arkansas.

On the first and third Sundays, Mother played for "General Day" at her church, Cherry Hill Baptist Church, in Moscow, Arkansas. On second and fourth Sundays, she played at Shiloh AME Church at Tamo. Three siblings joined Shiloh AME church, and my oldest sister joined Cherry Hill Baptist Church. However, all were baptized in Noble Lake. Cherry Hill was the church home for the Rodgers Family, according to Uncle Pearl Rodgers, my mother's brother. He said, "I joined Cherry Hill Baptist Church in 1923. Alma got religion on September 9th, and Cousin Juanita Howard joined September 13, at a church revival."

We were ecumenical. When our family moved to Pine Bluff, so the children could attend school nine months of the year, we held memberships at St. John AME Church and First Missionary Baptist Church. St. Andrews Episcopal Church, where I sometimes attended, was two doors away from our home. We respected, worshiped, and participated in activities at all churches. There were certain terminologies common to most Black churches that one knew if you were *"Raised in a Black Church."*

In St. Louis, I joined Hopewell Baptist Church. In St. Paul, Minnesota I was married in a Lutheran church and later joined Pilgrim Baptist Church. In Pine Bluff, Arkansas, I married the Pastor of Faith Presbyterian Church, Rev. Hayward Henry, and upon relocating to the State of California, I joined St. Paul AME Church in San Bernardino. Our children attended Catholic as well as public schools.

Quartet singing was prevalent in rural areas. As a child, I recall "quartet singing" at church on Sunday evenings was held as a fundraising activity. The quartets sang acapella, and the harmony was amazing. It was the Sunday night quartet singing and collections that enabled small churches to pay the bills. Quartets traveled far and wide with their thigh-slapping foot-stomping spirited music. It was also a social time for the younger set, who hung outside of the church building as much as possible.

Cousin Theo Rodgers was a member of the well-known, well-traveled "Spiritual Five of Pine Bluff," which celebrated their 60th year, according to an article in the Pine Bluff Commercial Newspaper. The quartet is the subject of a video documentary, *Ain't That Good News*, by two University of Arkansas at Pine Bluff Music professors, Dr. Michael Bates, and Professor Ernest Lamb. "The Spiritual Five has been a traffic stopper for quite some time."

Returning from a performance in Hot Springs, Arkansas, the group stopped at a drive-in to get food, but the owner came out to ask what they were doing there – what they wanted. The Spiritual Five explained that they were a singing group and then they started singing on the spot. Traffic stopped to listen, and the group made more money from donations on the street corner in Sheridan than they had made in Hot Springs. "They got free food, too," Professor Lamb said. The story illustrates that "gospel music is a way to bring people together."

Mother's cousin Theo was born April 16, 1922, to James and Mary Rodgers in Tamo, Arkansas. He passed in Pine Bluff, Arkansas in March 2016 at age 93. He was a member of the Spiritual Five Quartet for 60 years. Music was always a cornerstone of the family. Both Mom and Dad were singers, and Mother was a pianist.

Very few churches had pianos, consequently, choirs sang acapella using Do-Re-Mi syllables and "shaped notes." The "Do, Re, Mi, Fa, Sol, La, Ti, Do" syllables were popularized by Julie Anderson in the movie "The Sound of Music." However, rural families were using this "rote" type of singing at the turn of the century. I inherited the book, *The Rudiments of Music*, by James Murray copyright 1888, from my mother. It was noted in this book that each note had three names: a pitch name, a numerical name, and a syllable name. Consequently, even one-half steps of sharps and flats could be denoted by name, such as on an ascending scale ~ Do, Di, Re, Ri; or on a descending scale ~ Do, Ti, Te, La, Le, etc. The leader gave a pitch, each singer sang his/her pitch, and the singing began, with beautiful harmony. A popular book for "shaped notes" was *The Gospel Pearl*, used by many acapella choirs.

There were a few staunch families that kept the small churches operating in the rural areas. Some families at Shiloh AME Church in Tamo, were the Daltons, Nish Crawfords, Wallace Redds, Harry Halls, Columbus Strains, Aaron Sheltons, and the Roy Collins families. Reminiscing in 2016 with Claudine Goods and Ellistene Collins, we recalled the necessity to memorize and recite poems for numerous churches, school, and community events. We had no choice. Mother had a wealth of resources so that she always made teaching and learning interesting. Presentations on life situations were made understandable by utilizing various mediums, such as the caricatures in the Book of Proverbs.

Mother was always business-oriented. When Shiloh AME church was abandoned, a warranty deed in book 283, page 362, states that the Shiloh Abandoned Property Committee of the Central Arkansas Conference of the African American Episcopal Church of the 12th Episcopal District sold the property to Mrs. Alma E. Dalton. This deed was signed on August 4, 1959, and was an effort to keep Blacks in control of the property. Shiloh was originally named Allen Temple African Methodist Church of Tamo. The community church was also the community center. When Merrill High School burned, in approximately 1937, classes were held at St. John at AME Church, located one block from the high school, and at St. Paul Baptist Church, on the east side of Pine Bluff.

Baptism in rural areas was a community event to which residents traveled from miles and miles to attend. The baptism was usually held in a lake, a bayou, a river, or other outdoor naturally formed body of water. When one became about 11 to 13 years old, it was expected that after attending Sunday School, Church, and religious activities from birth, one should be about ready to publicly profess a belief in God. Consequently, churches held nightly weeklong church revivals. Those who were ready to "get religion" sat on a "Mourner's Bench." Religious believers would pray for the mourners to "crossover" and be saved. There would be lots of singing, praying, and preaching each night. As a mourner was "saved," the convert sat on another seat. At the end of the week, the number of mourners was counted, and a date was set for the baptism. The date was announced and the whole community, and surrounding churches, turned out for the baptism. For example, I professed religion at a revival at Cherry Hill Baptist Church, Moscow, Arkansas.

I was baptized in Noble Lake about three miles north of Moscow. The Sunday of my baptism, the converts met at a house across the highway from Noble Lake. We dressed in white gowns with white handkerchiefs or headscarves tied around our heads and we were led across Highway 65 South to Noble Lake. About 10 feet into the lake stood two ministers prepared to dip each convert under the water. As each convert was singularly led into the lake, one minister raised his hand skyward and proclaimed, *"I baptize you my sister/ brother in the name of the Father, the Son, and the Holy Ghost."* He then placed his hand over the nose and mouth of the convert, and *"whoosh,"* both men dunked the convert into the water, backward, until completely submerged. When the convert came up out of the water, there were different reactions. Some individuals shouted, some flailed their arms, and reactions differed with different people. Some of us sang a little song that was expected by some listeners. The little song was,

"I'M JUST SO GLAD DON' KNOW WHAT TO DO. I DONE DIED ONE TIME, AIN'T GOT TO DIE NO MO'. I ASKED THE LORD IF I HAD RELIGION TO LET ME FEEL IT DOWN IN MY SOUL. I'M JUST SO GLAD DON KNOW WHAT TO DO. I DONE DIED ONE TIME, AIN'T GOT TO DIE NO MO'."

This little singsong was a testimony to the fact that one had crossed over from sinner to believer. The chant was sung until the baptized individual reached the shore where the convert was covered with a towel or blanket and escorted back to the house across the highway. Very often, new clothes awaited the baptized individual.

After the baptism, there was usually a celebration with food, congratulations, and much backslapping. As said earlier, a baptism and a funeral were two big community events attended by friends, acquaintances, and non-acquaintances from miles around. People came on foot, on horses, in wagons, in automobiles and trucks. It mattered not who knew whom, people lined the banks of the river or lake to cheer on the new converts to Christianity.

XI

PERSONAL TRIALS & ADVERSITIES

The Baffling Feet amazed everyone. When I was approximately second or third grade, and attending Merrill School in Pine Bluff, Arkansas, I developed a disease on both feet that has continued throughout my lifetime. The ailment has received various diagnoses by various doctors. It appeared to be some kind of fungus by the symptoms, although to this day we do not know what it is, and I no longer seek answers.

In the summer, water blisters formed on the bottom of my feet. These blisters would burst and become sores. This occurred whether we pricked the blisters with a sterilized needle (burnt with a match) or let the blister develop on its own. Every summer I could not walk because of the painful sores. Dad carried me around like a baby until I became too large to carry. I have crawled on the floor with knee pads, used wheelchairs, and walked with crutches in order to be mobile.

My parents took me to numerous doctors in Pine Bluff, Little Rock, and even the Skin and Cancer Hospital in Hot Springs, Arkansas seeking a solution. I was told in Hot Springs that I had already received too many x-ray/radiation treatments, and they would not admit me for treatment. We heard of a medical training hospital in St. Louis, Missouri for Black populations. At that time, all medical facilities were segregated. In Pine Bluff, the Davis Hospital was for White patrons, and the Links Hospital, founded by the Flowers Family, served the hospital needs of "Negro" residents. Likewise, both Black and White doctors practiced in segregated facilities and offices.

In the summer of 1947, we drove to St. Louis to seek treatment for my feet. I was admitted to The Homer G. Phillips Hospital. I remember one treatment involved a big oval-shaped device at the foot of the bed over which the bed linen was draped. There was also some type of light fixture and treatment involved. After approximately two months, I was healed sufficiently to return to Pine Bluff to School, but I had to travel back and forth every month via train to St. Louis for outpatient treatment.

By midyear of 1948, because of the expense of the travel, Mom, Dad, and family decided that I would enter school in St. Louis and stay with Uncle Felton and Aunt Perlina Rodgers. Vashon and Sumner High Schools in St. Louis would not admit me in the middle of my junior year, but Washington Technical High School took me on the premise that I would remain the next school year and graduate. Thankfully, I did not get held back a grade, and I graduated in the Class of 1949 from Washington Technical High School in St. Louis, Missouri, instead of Merrill High School, in Pine Bluff, Arkansas. I walked across the stage on crutches to receive my high school diploma and entered the hospital the next day for intensified treatment of the recurring sores.

In September 1949, I returned home and entered AM&N College in Pine Bluff. During the preceding years of illness and home confinement, I did not get held back a grade because lesson assignments were sent to my home by the teachers. I studied, returned the assignments, and passed all classes. Additionally, my sister Velma was in some of the same classes due to her losing a grade one year because of illness. Also, I had received a double promotion from the fifth to the seventh grades.

A lady from New York told Mother of similar previous problems she had. She found that by keeping her feet completely dry, she was able to control the infections. From that day forward, water never was put on my feet, and I have been able to walk each year. Taking a bath has been a challenge, but since 1949, my feet have not been submerged in a bathtub. I could never take a shower, and a procedure had to be devised to enable me to sit in a tub for a bath.

My marriage in 1951, and the move to the colder climate of St. Paul Minnesota, also added to the healing and control process. In each city to which I moved, I always sought medical treatment. Dr. Karon in St. Paul prescribed an ointment that worked very well with the dry climate and treatments, and there were no more summer outbreaks.

Eighteen years later, upon return to Pine Bluff, I ordered the medication via mail from St. Paul until the medicine was taken off the market. Seeking medical help, a Pine

Bluff doctor prescribed an occlusion, and the blisters began to reappear. I discontinued the treatment and have since refused any treatment that involved moisture on my feet. Instead, I have dealt with the corns and calluses that formed probably as a result of the lack of moisture. Over the years I cleaned my feet with alcohol.

During the years of affliction, many treatments were tried. One doctor had me soak my feet in a solution, save it and use the same solution again. The infection began to spread to the top of my feet, and my hands. That treatment was discontinued. Another doctor used an ointment that drew infection to the surface without allowance to clean properly. One could enter the front of the house and smell my feet in the back. That treatment was discontinued. Another doctor suggested my parents agree to amputate both feet. The response was a resounding "No!" His advice was no longer sought. At times the pain was so intense, that when confined to the bed at home on the farm, I cried that if I had a weapon, I would try to cut off my feet.

My physical ailment was another reason for the decision for Mother to "move to town" and stay in Pine Bluff with the children, while Daddy lived on the farm weekdays. The house at 121 N. Oak Street was arranged so that the living room, dining room, and back porch were down the center of the house, with two bedrooms and kitchen on one side, and two bedrooms and bathroom on the other. Our parents always arranged for my brother to have his own bedroom, and the girls had their rooms. At one point, we temporarily rented a bedroom to a wonderful couple, Father Roper and his wife, who lived in Forest City, Arkansas. Father Roper was the Pastor/Rector of the St. Andrews Episcopal Church two doors away on the corner. Mrs. Roper was an artist and held drawing classes for the neighborhood children. It was under Mrs. Roper that I learned to draw a railroad track creating the illusion of fading into the distance. We always loved attending the drawing classes.

It seems that everyone in the area knew of my affliction and had suggestions for a remedy. However, we eventually found that I could not remain in the south in the summer, until the advent of air conditioning. When traveling, I could only use bathtubs that afforded leverage on the sides to raise my body into and out of the water with my arms and elbows. The depth of the tub for maneuverability was also a factor. My feet were always kept above the level of the water in a bathtub.

Dishes were washed with rubber gloves and, my five children were always bathed with rubber gloves. Not knowing exactly what the ailment was, or if it was contagious, we always treated it as if it could be contagious. I have never walked barefoot or been able to wade or swim in the water - although my sign is Aquarius, the water bearer. When we lived in Minnesota, we owned a motorboat, and boated on the St. Croix River in Wisconsin, and elsewhere. My husband carried me from shore to boat if he could not maneuver close enough to prevent my stepping in water.

XII

NORTH TO MINNESOTA

A most important extra-curricular activity at AM&N College was participation in the college choir. As a second soprano, I had the pleasure of traveling with the choir during my sophomore year. The Choir Director, Mr. Ariel Lovelace asked if I could get ready to travel. My sister, Velma, who was a tailoring major, quickly made the required formal gown, we made all arrangements, and I had the honor of traveling north with the choir.

While in the choir, I met a second tenor who appeared to be "Mr. Wonderful." Lawrence Hampton was a returned soldier continuing his education. After two years of study at AM&N College, in August 1951, I moved to St. Paul, Minnesota, and married my college sweetheart, Lawrence Hampton. Larry's brother was a chef cook on the Great Northern Railroad, and Larry worked on the railroad during the summers.

I intended to begin my studies at the University of Minnesota. However, we began a family. It was 18 years later, the loss of our oldest child, and intervening experiences and decisions, that I took the four remaining children back to Arkansas, and re-entered college in 1969, at age 38, a single parent, with four children to support.

Right away, following our marriage in St. Paul, we sought to own our own home and purchased our first house at 848 Fuller Avenue. The house was strategically located two blocks from a main thoroughfare and bus line, University Avenue; one-half block from the Maxfield Elementary School; a grocery store was located on the corner, and we were three blocks from Pilgrim Baptist Church where we established our church membership. Neighbors on one side were Mr. and Mrs. Floyd Barr, and on the other were an older couple, Mr. and Mrs. Fred Shuck.

This Southern Girl in The North required an adjustment. We had a nice but relatively small house with three bedrooms, a living room, a dining room, a kitchen, and a full basement. In the backyard, we had a pear tree and planted a garden for fresh vegetables. Mr. Shuck, my neighbor, called me "country" because of the garden, but the next year he planted a garden and showed me how to pick off the "suckers" to produce larger tomatoes.

My Southern farm training guided my food preservation and survival activities in the North. I froze vegetables, fruits, and most foods. A farmer who sold eggs in town also sold cracked eggs at a much-reduced price. For cooking purposes, I cracked those eggs, stirred, and froze them in ice cube trays. Bread products were purchased from day-old bakeries and frozen. When slightly heated in plastic bags, the bread appeared to be freshly baked.

The children were active in church and school, singing in youth choirs, reciting poetry on programs, playing piano duets, participating in Boy and Girl Scout Organizations, and other social activities. At seven and six years old, Angelo and Alvia sang two duets at Maxfield Elementary School, accompanied by their mother, that "brought down the house." The duets were "There's a Hole in the Bucket," and "Shoo Fly Don't Bother Me." Alvia and Angelo also played piano duets.

Both Larry, who sang tenor, and I, a soprano, sang in the choirs at Pilgrim Baptist Church. I was sponsored by the Young Women's Choral Group, under the direction of Mrs. Louella Taylor, and assisted by my husband, to hold a concert on April 26, 1957. We were very active in church and school activities. Our first automobile was a two-tone green 1953 Oldsmobile hard-top convertible, purchased after the home was established. We added a second car, a black 1951 4-door Ford, on which the children later learned to drive a stick shift.

Larry worked on the Great Northern Railroad as a waiter, and his brother, Tallie Hampton was a chef cook. I have always been a determined individual, and one Christmas Eve when Larry was out on the railroad and had refused to purchase a Christmas tree, after dark, I walked two blocks to a tree lot on University Avenue and dragged a tree down the street and put it in the front window. I could not accept the idea of the children waking up without a Christmas tree on Christmas morning. To witness their eyes light up was worth rectifying the friction between their mother and father.

Railroad men had a standing joke about unfaithful wives, I was always faithful to my husband, but jealousy frequently reared its ugly head. Larry later obtained a different job, a Draftsman for the Buckbee-Mears Company in St. Paul for many years. He was no longer working on the railroad, but the consuming jealousy continued and escalated.

Discrimination reared its ugly head in Minnesota - as far north as one can go in the United States of America. Even there, the Southern Girl who went North experienced discrimination. An advertisement in the *Help Wanted* section of the *St. Paul Dispatch* indicated jobs available in Montgomery Ward. Having graduated with a clerical emphasis from Washington Technical School, and one of the fastest typists in the senior class, I felt confident I could pass any test administered. I filled out an application and waited to take the test. Other applicants came, were called back to take the test, and left. After seeing this pattern for a while, I inquired when I would take the test, I was told that were no more openings. When I returned home, I called and was told to "come on out" that there were plenty of jobs. I did not press the issue because we were contemplating moving.

I obtained employment at the St. Paul Public Library, and while working in the circulation department, the position of Head of the Circulation Desk became available. I was asked to train a Caucasian individual for the position, and I had previously trained someone for a promotion. After several discussions about the position, I offered my resignation. I was subsequently promoted to Head of the Circulation Desk. It was there that I heard about "loneliness at the top." Ms. Glenn, the stereotypically little old white-haired spinster librarian, told me that it was "lonely at the top"; I did not fully understand what she meant at that time but have since found that to be a true statement in many cases. Ms. Glenn, who lived with her unmarried sister, totally immersed herself in the library. She was the one who said that, as a librarian, she may not know everything, but she should know where to find the information.

XIII

COUNTRY LIVING

In 1961, we purchased a larger house in suburban Woodbury, Minnesota. It had a living room, family room, four-bedroom, full basement, walk-out rambler that sat on five acres of land. The house sat on a hill with a driveway that was approximately one-half block long. This proved to be rather challenging in the Minnesota winters. However, daughter Alvia relates that some of her fondest childhood memories are of sliding down the front hill in the snow on a saucer. She also said she enjoyed trudging down the long driveway when the school had to close early because of snowstorms. We entered the downstairs basement door by the garage, consequently, shoveling snow was always a priority.

My son Lawrence fondly recalls the oblong-shaped flower garden on the front lawn that could be seen on the hill from a half-mile away. It was very colorful with red salvia planted behind white petunias. Sometimes I added snapdragons, yellow marigolds, and other colorful flowers. It was his job to water the flowers, and as a result, Lawrence loves flowers and has a gorgeous backyard today with a strong emphasis on ambiance.

We also planted "truck patches" of corn, black-eyed peas, cucumbers, popcorn, white potatoes, and other popular vegetables. People stopped by to comment on the okra, which they had not seen growing since they left the south. We also planted peanuts but decided they were not worth growing in that climate. It was here that I drove a tractor because husband Larry was too slow setting up the rows to plant. Like the little red hen, I did it myself. The rows were crooked but at least the garden was planted. We grew enough to even sell produce - especially fresh corn and tomatoes, and our freezer was kept full of food. Larry was from Holly Grove, Arkansas and we both were "earth people."

"All That Shines Is Not Gold" is a true statement. When we moved to the all-White Woodbury Township, we retained our membership and participation in the choir at Pilgrim Baptist Church in St. Paul. Larry and I joined Pilgrim Baptist Church shortly after our marriage in 1952. The pastor was the Rev. Floyd Massey. When seeking a church to join, I visited the St. James AME Church but found the music insufficiently spirited. I liked the quality and presentation of music better at Pilgrim Baptist Church. Music has always been the main factor when seeking a church home. Both Larry and I sang in the senior choir, and I sang with the Young Women's Choral Group. This group sponsored us in a concert in 1957. Three of the ladies were godparents for our children. The director, Mrs. Louella Taylor, and husband Mr. Benjamin Taylor were Angelo's godparents, Mrs. Vashti Ransom and Mr. Samuel Ransom were Alvia's godparents, and Mrs. Knott and Mr. Moses Knott were Del's godparents, and Mrs. Ida Hicks and Mr. Joe Hicks were Lawrence's godparents.

Membership in the choir and various organizations required meetings midweek and weekends. For choir rehearsals, the children were usually left at home on our four-bedroom five-acre site. This was not good. Consequently, we decided to join a local church. We joined the Woodbury Baptist Church, and we were the only African American family in the area. Larry and I both sang in the choir. The pastor was the Rev. Anthony Fiene.

The children were quite active in church and at school. Angelo, the oldest child, was a gifted musician and was featured in school concerts. He even had a musical composition revised especially for him to play at a concert. He was featured on the front page of the local newspaper. We were active parents, and I was secretary of the St. Paul Park Band Parents organization. We were the ideal couple to outsiders, but all was not happy at home. Angelo had some difficulty with physiological and social adjustment.

We removed Angelo from the public school and enrolled him in St. Thomas Academy in West St. Paul - a Catholic all-male military preparatory school for boys. Our daughter, Pam, was enrolled in Montessori School. It was located next door at the "Visitation High School," a Catholic School for girls. Meanwhile, Alvia and Del were enrolled at Oltman Jr. High School and St. Paul Park Jr. High School. I worked as a Library Assistant at St. Thomas Military Academy to help defray the expenses of the two private schools.

I began to have a weird dream that something was chasing me. Jumping from rooftop to rooftop, tree to tree, under stairs and porches, hiding behind doors, I could never see what was chasing me. Twice, when I could not escape and was about to be caught, I would awaken. After the death of my son Angelo at age 15, I never had that dream again. It apparently was a warning dream that I was not to have interpreted.

Angelo Jerome Hampton was born on February 14, 1952. Angelo died of a self-inflicted gunshot wound on January 2, 1968. The funeral was held at Woodbury Baptist Church in Woodbury, Minnesota on a very cold day. Angelo was a student at St. Thomas Academy, a private, Catholic military school in Mendota Heights, Minnesota – a suburb of St. Paul, Minnesota. Angelo had been the Lead Trumpet Player in the band and was always sent to play taps at funerals. St. Thomas Academy provided an honor guard for Angelo's funeral.

St. Thomas Military Academy's sister school was "Convent of the Visitation School," also known as "Visitation." Visitation, a private Roman Catholic School for girls, was co-ed pre-K to 6 grades. My daughter Pamela Jeanne attended Montessori school at Visitation, adjoining St. Thomas Academy. It was the death of Angelo that shaped my educational future and my resolve to enter the field of counseling. I did not foresee the impending death of my son and, consequently, could not save him. I determined that perhaps I could save another youth who felt unable to cope with life's traumas.

My marriage had become a very physically abusive, violent situation, so when Larry and I could not effectively communicate and I dreamed that we lost my second son, I put the remaining four children in our 1958 Oldsmobile and headed to the farm in Arkansas. Seeing that I was determined to leave, Larry drove as far as St. Louis and then returned to Minnesota, while I drove to Arkansas. Upon my return to Arkansas, I reentered AM&N College in 1969, at age 38, a single parent, with four children to support. The intent was to try a trial separation from my husband.

Living in Arkansas was a culture shock for my children. In the City of St. Paul, Minnesota, when we left our immediate community, the environment was mostly White populated. Woodbury Church and their schools were all-White environments. The move to Arkansas placed my children in a predominantly Black environment and they were forced to make immediate adjustments.
The children were enrolled in school, participated in bands, athletics, and activities, and adjusted well, under the circumstances. They were part of an extended family in Arkansas. Husband Larry came to Arkansas for Christmas. An older snuff-dipping male tenant on the farm, Mr. Banister, met Larry and said: *"Ms. Mildred, That's a mean man. That man don't mean you no good...That's a mean man."* Seeing no change in Larry's attitude, and I was safe in Arkansas with my children, I filed for a divorce. Everything that was in Minnesota remained there.

I have often wondered how my youthful maturity may have impacted my life, children, and family. I had led a sheltered life; married at 18; had my first child, Angelo, at 19 in 1952; my next child, Alvia, was born in 1953; and son Del was born 11 months later in 1954. Husband Larry was out of town much of the time consequently I was virtually a single parent with three babies for a number of years. I conserved by growing gardens, sewing the children's clothes by hand, and implementing other thrift measures. I was 1,000 miles from my family in Arkansas and had to grow up quickly.

XIV

THE VILLAGE

The Tamo farmhouse became a village with three families living in the three-bedroom farmhouse. When brother Ulysses and wife Louise were remodeling their home on Main Street in Pine Bluff, they and their two sons, Glen and Ulysses IV stayed on the farm. An arsonist torched the house that was being remodeled, and they had to build a new house, causing them to remain on the farm longer than anticipated.

Sister Velma, husband Jack, and daughter Jacqueline, likewise were staying on the farm as their historic house in Pine Bluff was also being remodeled. Then Mildred came with her four children: Alvia, Delano, Lawrence, and Pamela. An Ethiopian African Proverb states: *"No matter how full the hen house, the hen finds a place to sit."* Having watched a hen force her way into a sitting position among crowded chickens, I know this to be a true statement.

Every member of all three families either worked or attended school 20 miles away in Pine Bluff. My brother was a music professor at AM&N College, which later became The University of Arkansas at Pine Bluff. My sister worked in registration at the University, and I was a student, worked as a library aide, and worked as a secretary in the music department of AM&N College. This was one of the Historically Black Colleges (HBCs) of the South which took students, regardless of test scores and graduated them into the world as trained scholars and contributing citizens.

All the children were involved in activities at their schools, whether in the band, the track team, debate, basketball, orchestra, or choirs. They all participated in various events and organizations. Consequently, when a car left from the farm going to Pine Bluff, the children had to be in a car and would be delivered to their various schools. Pam was a drum majorette at Carver Elementary and a cheerleader at Merrill Jr. High School. Lawrence played baritone horn in the band at Southeast Jr. High School and ran Track at Pine Bluff High School, while Alvia and Del were active in the Merrill High School and Pine Bluff High School bands and orchestra.

One would ride in whatever car that was traveling north to get you to work or school on time. The "last car" traveling south at the end of the day was always announced. "Last car leaving, all aboard!" After work and extracurricular school activities, one rode in whatever car was traveling south at that time. When a car moved, we all moved to various destinations. It was truly a "it takes a village to raise a child" situation.

The village was successful, and each family moved out of the farmhouse as their accommodations were ready to occupy. As their projects were completed the families vacated the farm. My brother moved back to Pine Bluff and when my sister's home was completed, they too moved back to Pine Bluff. At the same time, my children and I moved to Pine Bluff in an apartment that I had been seeking. Ironically my nephew, Milton Carl Henderson who had been attending Wayne State University in Detroit, Michigan was graduating and wanted to return to Arkansas. As the three families moved to Pine Bluff, my nephew and family moved to the farm, bought the home lot, and became administrator of the farm, in addition to pursuing his professional career.

Aretha Franklin's gospel song, "Climbing Higher Mountains" was always a motivator. With the decision to leave Minnesota, I applied for a job in the John Watson Library at AM&N College, where I previously worked when enrolled as a student from 1949 to 1951. I received a telegram to Tower Drive in Minnesota: "12 MONTH CONTRACT APPROVED SALARY $4,764; 4 WEEKS VACATION. PLEASE ANSWER WIRE COLLECT AS SOON AS POSSIBLE MRS. J. PALMER HOWARD HEAD LIBRARIAN AM&N COLLEGE." Needless to say, I answered immediately. Fortunately, I had a job upon arrival in Pine Bluff. While working in the library at AM&N College, I decided to enroll part-time in school to complete my college education, at age 38, with four children to support.

Following a stint working full-time under Librarian Mrs. Julia Howard, I obtained a part-time secretarial position in the music department under Mr. Ariel M. (Pops) Lovelace so that I could attend school full time. I was already known in the Music Department. I was in the 1949 College Choir, Mr. Lovelace (Pops) knew the family, my brother was a professor in the music department, I was a music major, and Mr. Lovelace understood my desire to obtain my college degree. I obtained financial aid, enrolled in college full-time, worked part-time, and graduated from the University of Arkansas at Pine Bluff, mid-year in 1971, with a degree in Music Education.

My student practice-teaching was completed at Dial Junior High School under noted Choir Director, Mrs. Margaret Johnson. The expectation was that I would obtain a position as Choir Director in the Pine Bluff Unified School District. The position, however, did not become available when anticipated, and to support my family in the Summer of 1971, I was hired as a receptionist in the Office of the Superintendent of Pine Bluff Unified School District. I was told I was overqualified and should not want that job. However, we needed to eat, and I thought there may be some advantages to working in the Superintendent's office. While in that position, under Dr. Roy Scoggins, I typed the History of the Pine Bluff Schools, a book that is in the libraries of both the University of Arkansas at Pine Bluff (UAPB), and the Pine Bluff City Library, with the name Mildred Dalton Hampton prominently displayed.

A Choir Director and General Music teaching position became available in August at the newly created Southeast High School, and I was hired. Although previously told by naysayers that I would never be hired because of a long waiting list, and music positions are seldom available, I was hired. I had proven my willingness to work, proven my abilities, and my people skills. My next rung on the ladder to success had been attained.

Freedom of Choice was available so parents could decide where they wanted to enroll their children. Having been in all-White environments, I wanted my children to live the Black Culture and Experience. I enrolled them in Merrill High School.

While attending school, all of the children were involved in music, sports, and other activities at Merrill High School and Carver Elementary School. Alvia played saxophone in marching and concert bands, and flute in the symphonic band; Lawrence played baritone horn in the bands and ran track; and Pam played tenor saxophone in the bands, ran track, and was a seventh-grade cheerleader. Delano played bass clarinet in the band before returning to Minnesota. The segregated society demanded too much of an adjustment for Del to safely remain in Arkansas. He returned to St. Paul to live with his father and eventually lived with Mr. and Mrs. Paul and Bonnie Pitman and family in St. Paul Park, with whom he stayed until graduation from high school.

In Pine Bluff, after living a short time in an apartment at 123 North Oak St., which was adjacent to our original 121 North Oak St. home, we moved to a newly completed low-income housing unit, the 38th Street Apartments. We all went to school. Whoever arrived home first "put on the hotdogs." We stayed there for a year during which time I met the Pastor of Faith Presbyterian Church, Rev. Hayward Henry, who became my second husband. We briefly moved to his apartment in the Jane Oliver Apartments near the University until our new home was built on McFadden Road. It was a three-bedroom, living room, family room, brick home on an acre of wooded land, approximately two miles from the University.

The Saga of The Reverend was quite impactful. After my return to Pine Bluff, one day I was in the beauty shop getting my hair done and a gentleman came in for a manicure. He began to talk "trash" about my pretty eyes and other compliments. I did not respond and my beautician, Ms. Edna Anderson, said "Girl, talk to him." At his request, I gave him my phone number. When he left the beauty shop, I found that he was the unmarried Pastor of the local Presbyterian Church in Pine Bluff. We began to correspond.

Rev. Hayward Henry began visiting me when I resided in the 38th Street apartments. I made sure he always left my apartment at an early evening hour because, as I told him, I had children for whom I had to be a role model. My parents taught us strict moral values. After a courtship, Hayward asked me to marry him, and we began plans. I told him I must meet his family before any marriage could take place. He had often talked about where he lived in New Orleans. He also said he had two daughters from a marriage in Alaska, where his wife had died of cancer.

The day before we were to go to New Orleans, Hayward said the trip could not be made at that time. We rescheduled. The second time we were to go, the morning of the trip when Hayward arrived, he gave an excuse for not going to New Orleans. I gave him back the engagement ring and told him there would be no marriage until I went to Louisiana to meet his family. A third date was set, and we headed for New Orleans. When we arrived at Baton Rouge, instead of turning left toward New Orleans, Hayward turned right. I inquired and was told we were headed for Opelousas, Louisiana where his parents lived. When we arrived, surprisingly, Hayward's daughter was there visiting from New Orleans. However, it was a daughter whom he had never mentioned to me. As it turned out Anna was a child of a previous marriage, and Anna had two brothers. Her mother still resided in New Orleans. Needless to say, this was quite a shock. This family had never been mentioned to me. Anna said that there were also two other daughters someplace whom she had never met.

Hayward's brother, Johnny, who lived in Opelousas, also said that Hayward was 10 years older than he publicly pronounced. It was quite an eye-opening visit. I met Hayward's mother, father, brother, and two sisters who lived in nearby towns. It was a very friendly and receptive visit. However, I kept thinking "what else is there to know." After our marriage, I found that when I met Hayward, he was engaged to marry another lady in Pine Bluff, and the wedding was imminent.

We proceeded with our wedding on July 20, 1970, at Faith Presbyterian Church in Pine Bluff, where Hayward was the pastor. We moved into Hayward's apartment at the Jane Oliver Apartments, near the University campus, until our home was built on McFadden Road. At that time, the children with me were Alvia, Lawrence, and Pamela. Delano had returned to St. Paul, Minnesota to live with his dad. A family friend, Nannie McPherson said, "Girl, you looked uncertain even as you walked down the aisle." I replied, "Yes, I had doubts." Hayward oversaw the building of our brick three-bedroom, one-and-a-half-bath home on an acre of wooded land.

Hayward was a good husband to me, a good father to my children, and worked hard on the promises to provide a nice home for the family. We had a garden and even raised rabbits, chickens, and a calf, which was accidentally strangled. When the calf prematurely died, Hayward called my nephew, Carl Henderson, from the farm, and they quickly butchered the calf and preserved the meat. However, some very interesting quirks happened during the marriage when we resided on McFadden Road.

Lawrence tells of the time that Hayward convinced him they should dig dirt from the backyard and build a swimming pool. The dirt was placed in the front yard for a driveway. The driveway was built but a swimming pool was never constructed. Although Hayward professed to not be an alcoholic, he would almost continuously drink a six-pack of beer. The store was one mile away, and Hayward continuously made trips back and forth.

Hayward was always flamboyant and told me he was going to make me a bishop's wife. He was determined to become a bishop and had been affiliated with the AME Church at some point.

Hayward's scruples were sometimes questionable. A friend of my mother, a former teacher who had gone through the ranks of Black teachers obtaining credentials, had tried to contact Hayward several times. Mr. Elders, a member of the Presbyterian church, finally told me that Hayward had borrowed $500 from him. Mr. Elders thought I was in need and made the loan. I was absolutely furious and told Hayward he had better repay that loan immediately and never ever involve me in his schemes.

Hayward obtained a job as a Chaplain at Cummins Prison, about six miles south of the Dalton farm. One day, a lady knocked on our door on McFadden Road looking for Hayward. He had gone to the store for a six-pack of beer, to return shortly. We waited, and waited, and when Haywood did not return the lady said she was there to ask him about the money she had given for Hayward to help her brother get out of prison. Hayward did not return home until the lady left. He denied knowing anything about her comments.

During the summer, my brother, who was a professor at AM&N College (now the University of Arkansas at Pine Bluff), obtained a summer job at Cummins Prison. One day he asked me if Hayward was going to work each day. Puzzled, I said, "Yes, he leaves every morning for work.

My brother said, "I had better share something with you just in case there are repercussions." It turned out that Hayward had lost his job but had failed to share that with me.

Hayward told me he had accepted a job in Mississippi and would come home on weekends. He wanted me to go with him, but I would not leave a stable job at The University, my degree, or uproot the children to pursue instability. During the time that Hayward was in Mississippi, I had the opportunity to go to St. Louis, Missouri to work on my Master's degree. Lawrence was in the house on McFadden Road by himself because he wanted to stay in Pine Bluff and graduate with his peers.

Hayward's trips home became more infrequent. On one trip home, a neighbor told me he saw Hayward driving by the house and the neighbor was unsure of Hayward's intentions. Since I was away and Lawrence was alone in the house, and I had no intention of going to Mississippi, I decided to seek a divorce. I called Hayward's church in Mississippi and was told Rev. Henry was not available, but Mrs. Henry was there if I wanted to speak with her. I called the Dalton's Family legal counsel, Attorney George Howard, and asked him to prepare whatever papers I needed to get signed. I put Pam in the car and headed for Louisiana. Hayward's sister, Esther, who lived in Louisiana thought I was coming to get him. Instead, he signed the necessary divorce papers. The property was to be settled later. After spending the night, Pam and I headed back to Pine Bluff. I was officially divorced for the second time.

I continued the pursuit of my education to make a life for my children and me. Sometime later, my son Lawrence, told me that my nephew, Ulysses, saw Hayward Henry in Los Angeles, California walking down a church aisle with a lady on each arm. Ulysses was a recruiter for a local community college. Hayward was always a showman. He was very persuasive and could convince one that it was raining when the sun was shining. I received word, some years later, that Hayward was deceased. He remained flamboyant to the end.

Integration and Freedom of Choice was implemented in the public schools, however, even though Pine Bluff High School was an available choice, I wanted my children to experience the Black culture and enrolled them in Merrill High School which closed two years later. With the closure of Merrill High School, Alvia, Lawrence, and Pam attended and graduated from Pine Bluff High School. Lawrence was told by a White male counselor that he could never go to college and should just consider performing menial work. Carrying on the tradition, of "I can, and I will," Lawrence proved him wrong.

All of my children entered college and received a Bachelor of Science degree. Alvia finished at the University of Arkansas at Pine Bluff; Lawrence finished at Southern Illinois University at Edwardsville; Pam finished at Texas Woman's University in Denton, Texas; and in Minnesota, Delano finished at The University of Minnesota in Minneapolis. Pam also earned a Master's degree. They could, they would, and they did.

XV

BY ANY MEANS NECESSARY

In August 1971, a position opened at the newly created Southeast Junior High School, and I was hired to teach choral music and music education beginning in September 1971. I had proved my willingness to work, my abilities, and my people skills. Applicants on the waiting list for a music position remained on the list. The next rung on my ladder to success had been climbed. Our newly created eighth and ninth-grade choirs won awards and recognitions. Seventh-grade students learned about Opera and classical music by relating such music as the 1812 Overture to the theme song of the popular Lone Ranger television show.

After three years of teaching, my desire for further education resulted in researching and visiting the University of Missouri at St. Louis, and Southern Illinois University at Edwardsville. I visited both campuses and I was accepted and entered the counseling program at Southern Illinois University at Edwardsville (SIUE). I could not have accepted the opportunity without the support of my family. My son, Lawrence, chose to remain in the house on McFadden Road to graduate with his senior class at Pine Bluff High School. My brother, Ulysses Grant Dalton III, sister Velma Dalton Gilbert, and nephew, Milton Carl Henderson, provided oversight for Lawrence. My daughter, Pamela, went with me to St. Louis, enrolled in Normandy High School, and played tenor saxophone in the marching band. Pam played with the Normandy Band at the St. Louis Municipal Opera in a production of "Girl Crazy."

My oldest daughter, Alvia, was married, and my older son, Del, unwilling to accept the southern customs, had returned to Minnesota. My brother kept my piano and provided oversight for my son and home. The family village made it possible for me to continue my quest for higher education. Pam and I lived with my mother and stepfather in St. Louis while pursuing a Master's degree. I commuted to SIUE for evening classes, and taught in the Wellston School District, as a substitute teacher, every day that I wanted to work. Mother, an elementary teacher, worked in the St. Louis area, had materials for all grade levels, and a duplicating machine in the basement of their home. When a call to teach was received, grade-level materials were grabbed, and teaching was the order of the day. The principal of the elementary school where I taught was a graduate of AM&N College, so I felt "right at home."

"A Hand Up, Not A Hand Out" needed clarification throughout my experiences. A young African American male college student inquired in a class if I was in favor of "giveaways," such as food stamps. I related that I was the recipient of food stamps and fought to get them when I was in need. Upon graduation from SIUE, I had no job and no income. Having just earned my Bachelor's degree in June, there were no summer jobs available in Pine Bluff. I had signed a contract to begin work in September but needed to eat and feed my daughter during the summer. I explained this to the interviewer, however, I was denied. I explained to her that I was truthful, properly dressed, had paid taxes all of my life, and my parents before me. Now I needed a hand up and not a handout. I intended to get it. I tore up the contract (to be reinstated later) but I was still denied. I was determined to get food for my family for those two months. I contacted my Arkansas State Representative, Henry Wilkins III, a former Merrill School classmate. My case was reevaluated, and I received the food stamps.

There was a second occasion when I applied for food stamps and was denied. Having received my Master's degree, and signed a contract for the upcoming year, I returned to Pine Bluff from Southern Illinois University, unable to secure summer employment. I was denied food stamps and I called my State Senator, Knox Nelson. I followed his suggestions and received a call to be told that my application had been reevaluated. Upon receiving a paycheck on both occasions, I no longer accepted food stamps or a welfare check. While receiving food stamps, however, I was informed about welfare and the WIN program. I applied for welfare for one month because I had no income, could not find a summer job, and needed to pay my house note. As a result of being on welfare, the WIN program paid for my first year of employment as a counselor at the Watson Chapel Unified School District near Pine Bluff.

To the Inquirer I stated that "I believe in community services that render a hand-up in time of need. I am not in favor of continued hand-outs if the recipient makes no effort to better one's condition." While teaching a counseling class at Southern Illinois University, I related these experiences, and I was told by one of my White male students that I should not have fought for food stamps. I replied, "You should walk a mile in my shoes."

XVI

THE PAYOFF

Upon graduation from SIUE, I was hired as the first counselor for the 1,356 students at Coleman Middle School in the Watson Chapel School District of 3,840 students, 46.7% minority. While at Coleman Middle School, adjacent to Pine Bluff, I introduced new ideas to the area, such as *A Careers Day in April*, utilizing local community resources. This was a first in the State of Arkansas at the middle school level. Twenty-three firms and organizations presented approximately 40 career possibilities for the students. The *Coleman Peer Tutoring* Program (CPTP) was established in response to over 200 student requests for academic help. We established a *Visual Media Program* to address self-esteem awareness and *A Youth Summer Cultural Enrichment Program* for community youth.

The University assisted with a *Create-a-Drama Ensemble*, utilizing student and teacher participation, and the *University at Arkansas Pine Bluff (UAPB) Choir* was also presented in an assembly at the middle school. These positive projects were so effective, I was asked by the Jefferson County Superintendent of Education, Dr. Turner, to write an article. My first publication, *"Setting Up a Responsive Program in a Middle School"* was published in the April 1979 issue of <u>The Guidance Clinic</u>, by Parker Publishing Company, New York.

I wrote and submitted a proposal to the State of Arkansas Department of Education, February 1, 1977, to obtain funds under the Title IV, Part C section, to provide summer jobs for peer tutors of the Coleman Tutoring Program. It was funded, however, the Watson Chapel District Superintendent told me otherwise and negotiated for the $50,000 grant, without my knowledge. The Superintendent told me that the counselor position at Coleman School was terminated. Consequently, I immediately applied at AM&N College and was hired as a counselor with the Upward Bound Program directed by Mr. Leo Collins. I remained with the Upward Bound program until the University campus atmosphere, and the desire to emulate my brother motivated me to seek a Doctor of Philosophy (Ph.D.) degree.

I applied to the Department of Educational Psychology at Southern Illinois University Carbondale. Again, I was told that I was too old to return to college and compete with the younger students. However, one professor, Dr. Michael Altekruse, said "I will work with her." Dr. Altekruse was an excellent mentor and advisor, and I had the support of his colleagues as my advisory committee.

I am deeply indebted to Dr. Altekruse, Program and Dissertation Chairman, Dr. Harold Bardo, Dr. Seymour Bryson, Dr. Joseph Karmos, and Dr. Malvin Moore, for making it possible to add the suffix, Ph.D. to my name. Incidentally, Dr. Moore was a Pine Bluffian who previously taught tailoring at AM&N College and was my sister

Velma's Professor in Pine Bluff.

Many obstacles and distractions were encountered as an older female reentering the educational arena. My dissertation for the Ph.D. was entitled *"The Concerns of Black Reentry Females in Selected North Central Association Graduate Schools."* I changed my focus from school dropouts to a study of reentry females as a result of experiences encountered as an African American female in my trek for higher education. I believed that a minority woman who was a reentry student had additional concerns when compared to other populations. Data was extremely limited as I began this descriptive exploratory research. Researchers indicated that several studies on re-entry females had been conducted, however, Black female participation had been minimal or non-existent. The purpose of the study was to collect demographic information on Black re-entry females in graduate school, identify their needs, and determine utilization of institutional services. Re-entry referred to persons returning to the educational system after an absence of approximately five to twenty years. The subjects were female Afro-Americans; 30 and older; who had been absent from formal education a minimum of five years; and who were currently enrolled in graduate school. Seven North Central Association Graduate Schools participated in the study. The Black Re-Entry Female Survey (BREFS) was mailed to 270 students, of which 161 questionnaires were returned and analyzed by the Statistical Analysis System (SAS).

The data revealed that:

> *The "typical" Black re-entry female in the population surveyed was between the ages of 30 and 39; married; employed full time; enrolled in school part time; had one or two children; and made over $20,000. Descriptive comments indicated that the student re-entered school for self-fulfillment purposes; expressed a need for financial aid; experienced feelings of isolation and prejudices on campus; felt pressured by responsibilities and time constraints; and indicated minimal utilization of student support services. Based on comments of participants in this study, it is also suggested that special effort be made to employ more Black female faculty who can serve as role models and mentors.*

The Concerns of Black Re-Entry Females in Selected North Central Association Graduate Schools, 1983.

XVII

CONTINUING THE LEGACY

In order to continue my studies, again, my family was my fortress. While I was at SIUE, the way was paved for my son, Lawrence, to begin his college studies at Edwardsville. We were able to secure some scholarship and entry funds, but he had to work and earn money to support his education. He relates how he ate a lot of popcorn which, with a drink, will help fill an empty stomach. Lawrence was active and became editor of the *"The Harambee,"* the campus African American oriented newspaper. Lawrence was included in the 1978-79 edition of *"Who's Who Among Students in American Colleges and Universities,"* and in the 1979 edition of the *"Outstanding Young Men of America."* Lawrence graduated from SIUE in 1980 with a major in Political Science. While at SIUE, Lawrence met and married Joyce Chambers, also an outstanding student on campus. Later, Lawrence won a seat on the Little Rock, Arkansas School Board of Education.

Meanwhile, Pamela entered Texas Women's University (TWU) at Denton, Texas where she graduated in 1983 with a Bachelor of Science degree in Speech-Language and Pathology, received her Master's degree from Central State University in Oklahoma City, and moved, with her husband Charles, to employment in Dallas, Texas.

While at TWU, Pam received several academic scholarships, was a member of several honor societies, the National Student Speech-Language-Hearing Association, TWU Contemporary Gospel Ensemble, the NAACP, and was selected *Miss Essence*. She was published in the 1980 to 1983 editions of the *National Dean's List*.

Alvia, upon graduation from Pine Bluff High School, entered Ouachita Baptist College in Texarkana, Arkansas. She transferred and completed studies for a Bachelor of Science degree in elementary education in 1975 at AM&N College in Pine Bluff. After a stint as an Armed Services Wife, she worked in the Music Department at Grambling University in Louisiana. Later, she moved to Philander Smith College in Little Rock, Arkansas, and became a tenured teacher in the Little Rock Unified School District for 11 years. She moved to the Fort Worth, Texas School District where she worked as a tenured elementary school teacher. After working 35 years with the little children that she loved, she retired in 2016. When in college, Alvia was listed in *"Who's Who Among Students in American Colleges and Universities,"* and in later years was nominated and listed in *"Who's Who Among American Teachers."*

Delano entered Bethel College in St. Paul, Minnesota after graduating from high school. Recommended by his High School Choir Director, he applied and received a choir scholarship, where he sang in the Bethel College Choir under Dr. Robert Burglund. While completing his college degree, Del worked as a waiter at Bigelow's Restaurant in the Sheraton Midway in St. Paul. He was such a skilled craftsman that an article was written and published about him in the October 1982 edition of the *Minneapolis- St. Paul Magazine.* Del completed college studies at the University of Minnesota and worked for years in the computer technology field with American Express and Ameriprise. He was also a private entrepreneur with a computer business. Upon retirement, he was hired by the University of Minnesota as a *Master Gardener* teaching Agricultural Technology in the community.

Del is known throughout Minneapolis for his various gardens. In 2015, he entered Dahlia flowers in the Minnesota State Fair Show and the Bachman's Fall Dahlia Show, where he won 17 first-place ribbons, 13 second-place ribbons, and seven third-place ribbons. At the Bachman Show, three of his entries made it to the "Court of Honors."

Lawrence's backyard is a garden showplace, the flowers, vegetable garden, and fishpond, with the mountains as a backdrop, could not be more relaxing. Both Pam and Alvia always had gardens in their backyards from which they planted, cultivated, harvested, and prepared food for the table. The gardening skills learned in childhood paid dividends in adulthood, despite the vow to never work in a garden when they "grew up."

In June 1983, I received a Ph.D. from SIUC, and Pam received a Bachelor's degree from Texas Woman's University at Denton, Texas. On August 20, 1983, Pam married her childhood sweetheart Charles Ross, who also graduated from Northeast Louisiana University in 1983; and both immediately enrolled in graduate school at Central State in Oklahoma City.

It took the Village to make for a successful journey. While working on my Ph.D. in Carbondale, approximately 90 miles from St. Louis, there were many weekends that I visited my sister Vhaness. She was an elementary school teacher in the Normandy School District and known to be a master teacher. While a student at SIUC, I received an appointment as a full-time permanent substitute teacher in the Carbondale Elementary School District, which meant I had full responsibility for bulletin boards and classroom decorations in a fourth-grade classroom. Not having previous full-time teaching experience, I called on the master teacher. We bought and collected materials and spread them out on the floor in her three-story condominium. We designed, cut, and pasted to make bulletin boards and lesson plans. When I left Sunday afternoon for Carbondale, I was prepared to teach. My decorated classroom was the talk of the school. For instance, a giraffe the height of the wall was projected and traced on brown paper. The leaves that he ate from a tree were all words of encouragement and motivation. I had other decorative, eye-catching, and teaching bulletin boards and decorated walls.

I have always been interested in communities and diverse cultures. While teaching at Parish Elementary School in Carbondale, I invited culturally diverse speakers from

Southern Illinois University to share their culture with my students. The diverse countries included Switzerland, Kenya, Liberia, Israel, Palestine, and others. Help from my sister was help from a master teacher.

Vhaness studied under Mrs. Katherine Durvan, Professor in the Department of Education at AM&N College. The college was nationally known for producing great teachers. I was also fortunate enough to take one class under Mrs. Durvan. She was a strict no-nonsense professor who was consumed with much knowledge to impart. Both Mr. and Mrs. Durvan worked on the campus, as did many other families. Many students were successfully mentored by families at AM&N, a Historically Black College (HBC).

Both Vhaness and I were college dropouts. After two years of college, she moved to Chicago in 1951. After two years of college, I dropped out, moved to Minnesota, married, and began a family. Eighteen years later I returned to school, a single parent with four children to support. Having had those experiences, we both knew the importance of hard work and determination to succeed.

Mother was also known as an excellent teacher. Her favorite classroom saying was "let your walls talk." It was a family tradition to have decorated educational classrooms that taught messages and provided creative learning environments for students. In the Normandy School District, Vhaness "kept the walls talking" in the halls of the McKinley Elementary School in the Normandy School District.

The quote, "it takes a village," was very much applicable during this time. I was in Carbondale studying for a Ph.D., while Lawrence was in Edwardsville studying for his Bachelor's degree. There were many weekends that Lawrence and Joyce visited Vhaness, in Chesterfield, Missouri, and/or Mother in St. Louis, usually returning home with a full stomach and goodies. Vhaness lamented the fact that her money was limited, however, she loaded the cars down with usable items such as canned food, toilet tissue, and other household necessities.

While I was in Edwardsville studying for my Master's, Lawrence wanted to remain in Pine Bluff to graduate with his class. My brother, who was a professor at AM&N College, rented space in our McFadden Road house to some of his students, Sigma Phi Beta fraternity brothers who needed housing. We thought they would be housemates for Lawrence so he would not be in the house alone. However, Lawrence told me years later that he was very uncomfortable, almost afraid. He did not voice those opinions at the time. I was happy that others were in the house with him because on two occasions when Lawrence was alone, the house was broken into by ruffians who lived nearby. I was afraid for his safety. My brother provided oversight for my son and my home.

The "it takes a village" concept extended to my neighbors who notified me when Lawrence was driving too fast. On one visit home, Mr. Goldsmith stopped by to report that "Lawrence is driving too fast." When questioned, Lawrence, smilingly, admitted to "jumping the ditch" one day in our little Toyota Corolla station wagon to avoid hitting a school bus in his haste to get to class. At school, Coach Andrew "AC" Butler, his track coach, who also acted as a surrogate father for the track team, kept a watchful eye on Lawrence knowing that I was away in school.

Our Toyota Corolla station wagon provided transportation for the family when I was in Pine Bluff, kept Lawrence rolling when I was in Edwardsville, and provided transportation for Pam when she entered Texas Women's University in Denton, Texas. It finally "died" on the roadside during one of Pam's trips home.

The "Headquarters" when I made trips to Pine Bluff was with my sister. Sister Velma lived at 1205 W. 2nd St., located conveniently on the bus line and in the heart of Pine Bluff. Her home was a headquarters for family members. Brother U.G. lived at 3522 South Main Street, near the outskirts of town. Both homes were headquarters when the family came to town. Velma's house was a stopping point near the freeway, and she always had food prepared to eat. Whatever was not prepared would be cooked shortly. Aunt Louise, across town, was an excellent cook and the children knew there was always food at Uncle U.G. and Aunt Louise's house. Family gatherings were held at my brother's home who had a large one-story rambler, 3-bedroom, 3- bath, living room, dining room, family room, brick home with a large yard.

Velma's house was a two-story Victorian house that reminded me of fairy tales and should have been placed on the National Historic Register. However, discrimination still existed, similar homes owned by White residents in nearby blocks were placed on this preservation register and were eligible for renovation and preservation funds.

I idolized my brother, the oldest sibling, who truly took on the role of leader of the family. He was a leader from an infant sitting in my parent's 1920's roadster, to coordinating the Chancellors Ball at the University of Arkansas, to running for public office as Alderman and Justice of the Peace. I emulated his actions, selecting music as my major, teaching, and education as my profession, and obtained a Ph.D. following in his footsteps. The oldest and youngest siblings, "the bookends," earned the highest degrees in education. We all had special talents. Velma excelled as an entrepreneur with her Amway business.

Sister Velma was also an excellent seamstress and her major in college was tailoring. This gift was picked up by my daughter Alvia, who made all of the wedding gowns and dresses for her wedding to her second husband, Joe Page. She also made all of the gowns for her sister Pam's wedding to Charles Ross. While I was away in school, Alvia was the principal planner and coordinator for the wedding for Pam and Charles. Eight years older than Pam, Alvia assumed a "little mother" figure for Pam. When Pam, living in Arlington, Texas, was diagnosed with lupus, Alvia moved from Little Rock, Arkansas to Fort Worth, Texas, and began teaching in the school system there, to be near Pam.

When living in Pine Bluff as a child, church members were part of "the village." Mrs. Alberta Bradley was our beautician and Mr. Bradley was a repairman who kept our household appliances and plumbing working. Mr. Lewis Yancy owned a furniture store and always arranged convenient payment terms for purchases. His employee, Jimmy, was an excellent appliance repairman who kept the village serviced. Mr. and Mrs. Meadors owned and operated a service station that kept all of our cars working for three generations. Mr. Meadors also hired Lawrence for his first job at age 13. He rode his bike approximately eight miles each way from McFadden Road to and from the service station on Barraque Street in Pine Bluff. This was Lawrence's first valuable experience in learning work ethics, which paid dividends when Lawrence went to college and has aided him throughout his professional career. Other members of the village worked together to produce youth who were educated, hard-working, successful, and contributing citizens to our society.

Music and role models in our family and community permeated throughout our lives. Among influences at St. John AME Pine Bluff were Mr. and Mrs. Herman and Fannie Mitchell. Mr. Mitchell, a tenor in the choir, had a gospel music radio program. He was accompanied by Mrs.

Mitchell, an alto, pianist, and minister. In the early 1970s their daughter, Beth Mitchell, was a pianist for St. John's youth choir, which I directed when I returned from Minnesota. My daughter Alvia was also a pianist for the youth choir. Lawrence and Pam were in the choir and Pam was a soloist. My nephew Ulysses played drums and a cousin of Beth Mitchell, Bertram Green, played tenor sax. It was a family affair. There was some resistance from some older members of the church, however, I reminded them that in Psalms 150 we are exhorted to "Praise Him" with the sound of the trumpet, with the psaltery and harp, with the timbrel and dance, with stringed instruments and organ, and with the high-sounding cymbals. While performing at another church, the comment was made *"Y'all sound like sanctified folk,"* to which I replied, *"I think all of God's children should be sanctified."* I countered that it is better for youth to be in the church with their instruments than to be on the street corner with drugs and prostitution.

The Mitchell's niece, Maxine Vaughn, a longtime organist and pianist at St. John, is an excellent musician and accompanies me whenever I sing in the area. In later years, Beth Mitchell contacted me in California when she came to live with a sister. We hired Beth at the PAL Center where she worked for the Workforce Investment Act program. The tentacles of St. John Church reach far. She also joined St. Paul AME Church in San Bernardino where she was a very active pianist and soloist. My mother's first-grade student from Pine Bluff was in the ministry at St. Paul AME Church in San Bernardino, and now Pine

Bluff's St. John's youth choir pianist was also at St. Paul AME Church in San Bernardino.

Music still permeated within the families. When daughter Alvia moved to Fort Worth, Texas, she sang in the choir and played for the children's choir in her church. Pam played for the choir and the children in her church in Grand Prairie, Texas. Lawrence sang tenor in the youth choir in Pine Bluff and sang tenor in his church in San Bernardino.

The youth were also taught social graces. Pam and niece Jackie belonged to The Social and Arts Club in Pine Bluff where they were taught proper dress, table setting, etiquette, and other graces. Years later at the PAL Center, we taught proper dress and etiquette to a group of graduating seniors to prepare them to exhibit proper manners and behavior at their senior banquet

Nearing the end of my SIUC studies, I searched the *Chronicle of Higher Education* for employment and considered several institutions in Ohio, Georgia, New York, and California. Although the application deadline had passed, I applied to California State College, which became California State University at San Bernardino in 1984. I was contacted by Dr. Ernest Garcia, Dean of the College of Education, who flew to St. Louis Lambert Airport where we met for an interview. I was hired on the spot, although I had been warned many times that I was too old, jobs were too few, and I would never get a job in counseling. On the same trip, Dr. Garcia recruited Dr.

Margaret Cooney at the University of Illinois for a rehabilitation counseling position. We became staunch partners in the war against ignorance. Interestingly, at the first staff meeting in August 1983, Dean Garcia introduced myself, Dr. Mildred Dalton Henry, and another new professor, Dr. Henry Dalton.

Thus began the Westward Trek.

Affirmative Action and Education

"Affirmative action opens doors to opportunities that were previously closed to qualified women and people of color." - Elaine Jones, NAACP Legal Defense and Education Fund. It means taking positive steps to end discrimination, to prevent its recurrence.

General Colin Powell, in a commencement speech at Bowie State University, June 1996, said *"There are those who say that all you need is to climb up on your own bootstraps, but there are too many Americans who don't have boots, much less bootstraps. There are those who rail against affirmative action. They rail against Affirmative Action preferences while they have lived an entire life of preference."* ...*I don't speak about affirmative action from an academic sense, I speak from experience ... We created an environment where advancement came from performance and striving for excellence, and not from color or gender. But first, we had to open the gates to let people in."*

I have absolutely no doubt that I was offered a position of Assistant Professor in the School of Education position at California State University at San Bernardino (CSUSB) because of affirmative action and the lack of African American representation at that institution. At the time I was hired, in August 1983, no African American professor had obtained tenure, and consequently, no one had been retained as a tenured full-time professor in the School of Education at CSUSB. Through hard work and determination to attain tenure, I became the first African American to become tenured in the School of Education, the first to be promoted to Associate Professor, the first Full Professor, and the first African American in the School of Education to be awarded the status of "Professor Emeritus." This honor was bestowed by CSUSB President Albert Karnig.

The promotion to Full Professor was not without controversy and a battle with the previous administration. The University tenure committee did not recognize the importance of involvement with the community in which the university is located. Under the administration of Dr. Karnig, however, communications with, and providing services to, the community took on a new meaning.

California State University at San Bernardino and relocation to the Inland Empire community began another segment of *A Journey of a Lifetime* as we remembered the past to focus on the future.

Part 2 traces the California experiences, including California State University at San Bernardino; community involvement; pioneering community-based education, and the PAL Center; The Journey to the Motherland ~ Ghana West Africa; the naming of the Dr. Mildred Dalton Henry Elementary School by the San Bernardino City Unified School District; and the continuing legacy.

The Dalton Family 1800 A.D.

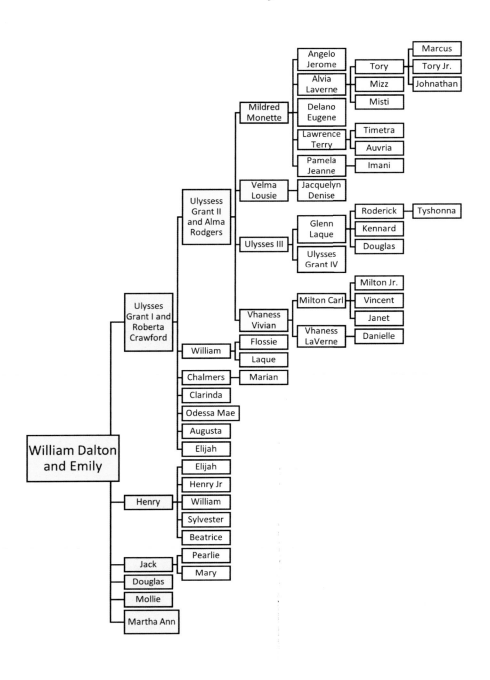

The Rodgers Family

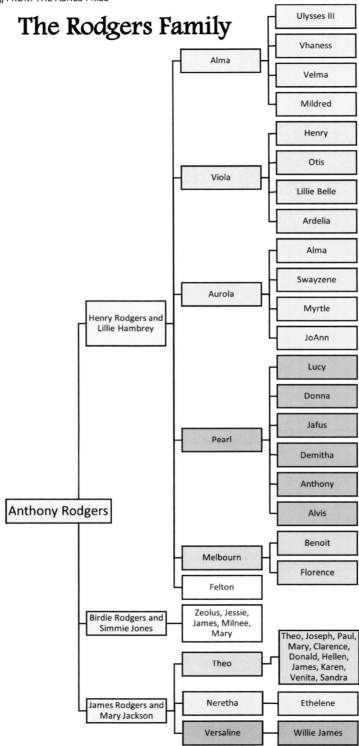

The Hambrey Family

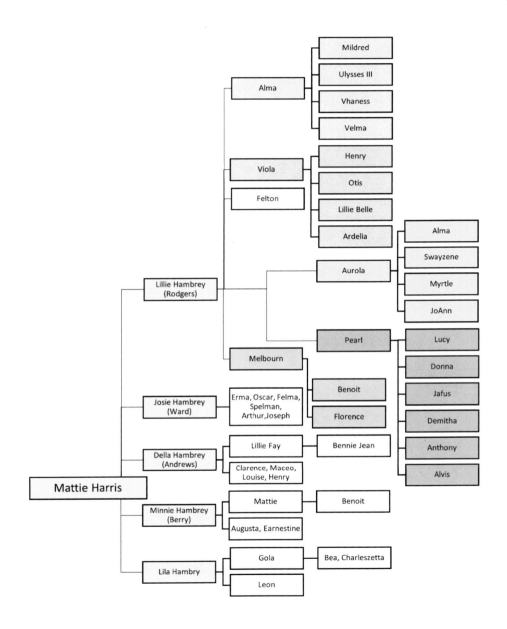

U. G. Dalton & Sons Cotton Gin
and General Store in Tamo,
Arkansas – about 1930.

Shotgun house in Pine Bluff,
around 1920s. Reportedly, one
could open front and back doors
and shoot through the house
without hitting anything.

Grandfather Henry Rodgers
and son Felton during hog
killing time in 1910.

A young boy picks cotton in
1938 for $.75 per 100 pounds
near Lake Dick - Altheimer,
Arkansas, where
grandfather, Ulysses Grant
Dalton, Sr. landed by boat
about 1900.

Beaus and Belles of Moscow in Dad's car
approximately 1924. U. G. Dalton and
Alma Rodgers in front seat. Genoa Wells
and Solomon Keith in back seat with
friends seated on the running board.

The Dalton brothers William,
Chalmers, Ulysses II, and
Cousin William Crawford, all
musicians, pose beside family
automobile.

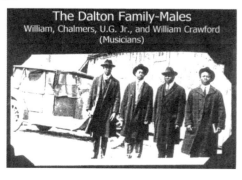

Mildred and husband Lawrence with children Angelo and Alvia in St. Paul, Minnesota Christmas 1953.

Angelo Jerome Hampton is a happy 2-year-old St. Paul, MN

Alvia and Angelo play piano duet at Maxwell Elementary School, St. Paul, Minnesota.

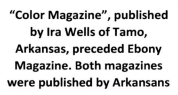

"Color Magazine", published by Ira Wells of Tamo, Arkansas, preceded Ebony Magazine. Both magazines were published by Arkansans

Angelo Jerome Hampton
First Chair Trumpet Player
St. Paul Park Jr. High School, St. Paul Minnesota

Junior Highs' to Present Band Concert

Angelo Hampton, son of Mr. and Mrs. Lawrence Hampton of Woodbury will be the featured trumpet soloist with the Jr. High Wind Band Ensemble.

A Wind Band Ensemble, made up of musicians selected from both St. Paul Park Jr. High and Oltman Jr. High will present a concert at the annual Midwinter Clinic of the Minnesota Music Educators Association, held in St. Paul's new Hilton Hotel this year. The Band will perform in the Grand Ballroom at 4:30 on Friday, February 17th.

The band will play some of the finest literature available for the concert band, including music from the Baroque and Classical eras, a contemporary Overture, outstanding marches and music of a lighter nature. A highlight of the program is a brilliant Trumpet Solo, this solo having been specially arranged with band accompaniment by Mr Budahl and played by Angelo Hampton, the band's 1st Trumpeter.

The Band is directed by Mr. Harold Lomenick and Mr. Monty Budahl. The Chief Clinitian and speaker at this two day clinic is Vaclav Nehlybel, a Hungarian refugee and a most respected composer of band music who now resides in New York City.

On Tuesday, February 14th at 8:00 P.M. in the St. Paul Park Jr. High Auditorium, the band will present the entire concert for the public. Tickets may be purchased at the door. They are 50¢ for adults and 25¢ for children.

Music Teacher and Director 9th Grade Choir at Southeast Jr. High School Pine Bluff, Arkansas

Daughter Pamela when a majorette at Carver Elementary School, Pine Bluff, AR. Band marched in AM&N College Homecoming Parades.

Pamela in Normandy HS Band, St. Louis, MO. Pam performed in the St. Louis Metropolitan Opera production of "Girl Crazy".

Carbondale, Illinois 4th grade bulletin boards teach students from the walls.

Mildred Dalton Henry with sister Velma Dalton Gilbert and sister-in-law
Louise Slack Dalton at AM&N College Football Homecoming Game.
Photo taken by famed photographer Geleve Grice.

Irma Ross, Pamela Hampton Ross, Mildred Dalton Hampton Henry

Alma Rodgers Dalton Gates

Ulysses Grant Dalton I

Ulysses Grant Dalton II

Mildred Dalton at 7 years old, somewhere in the crowd

Rev. H.M. Green stands with youth and other members in front of St. John AME Church in 1941. The building pictured had been in use since 1897 and was replaced in 1966. With a critical emphasis on facilitating affordable housing opportunities along with important work in civil rights, social activism, and spiritual instruction, St. John has made biblical teachings tangible and relevant for all, including "the least of these." (Courtesy of Connie Elkins Collection.)

Nicknamed "The Blue Vein Church", St. Andrews was two doors from Mildred Hampton's house

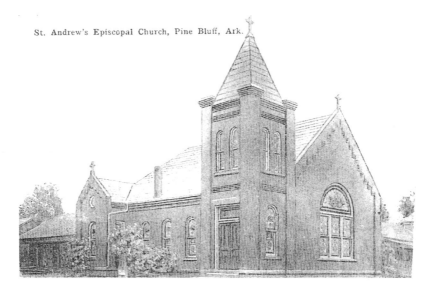

St. Andrew's Episcopal Church, Pine Bluff, Ark.

Many Faces to Success!

Ulysses Grant Dalton II:
Graduation Photo

Ulysses Grant Dalton II:
Band Photo

Ulysses Grant Dalton II:
Staff Photo

Photos provided by: University Museum and Cultural Center,
University of Arkansas at Pine Bluff

Del featured in St. Paul-Minneapolis, Minnesota Magazine

Del on 5-acre Tower Drive Home Woodbury, Minnesota

Thursday, Feb. 10, 1977   *The Daily Alestle*

BSA, SIP editor taking early career steps

By Angela Beal
For the Alestle

Lawrence Hampton, like many other students, is a freshman and a journalism major here at SIU. But what makes him unusual is that he is both editor of the Supplemental Instructional Program (SIP) newsletter and the Harambee, the Black Student Association's (BSA) bi-weekly supplement to the Alestle.

Hampton, an 18-year-old native of Pine Bluff, Ark., enrolled at SIU the summer of '76 and soon afterward was hired by Lula Lockett, program director of SIP, to become editor of the newsletter. During the fall quarter, the BSA hired him as editor for the supplement.

"When I was in high school I was known for blowing things out of proportion if something happened to me. I was sort of a joker. I'd tell the stories to my mother and after awhile, she suggested that I get on the school newspaper staff. I did. It was kind of a challenge between us," Hampton said.

While writing for the school newspaper in Arkansas, Hampton received honorable mention and a certificate from the Arkansas Press Association for writing an article about Judy Petty and Wilbur D. Mills running against one another for Congress. Hampton also received a certificate for writing a sports column.

Since writing for the Harambee, Hampton says, "I think it is a fabulous idea the BSA has come up with. It has a lot of potential, but I'm disappointed at times because I find a lack of response from the students. We need their support because without them it's nothing."

Now that he's found something that "makes me feel like I'm doing something worthwhile," Hampton said he hopes to someday write for a popular magazine like Playboy, and would also like to write a book.

"I'm not sure exactly what the book will be about, but it will probably be an autobiography. While working with a magazine like Playboy I hope to do some extensive traveling," Hampton said.

While most 18-year-old freshmen are still deciding what they want to do in life, Hampton has already chosen his career and is taking steps to reach his goals.

Lawrence featured in The Daily Alestle on February 10, 1977

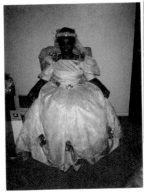

Alvia made her gown for wedding to Joe Page.

Alvia made the Maid of Honor Gown for Pam, all bridesmaids, and entire wedding.

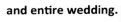

Del walking Alvia down the aisle at her 1992 wedding to Joe Page in Ft. Worth, Texas.

Mizz Turner, Auveria Hampton, Imani Ross, Misti Turner, Timetria Hampton

9 & 10 yr. old U.G. and Vhaness

Mizz and Misti Turner

Misti Monette Turner

Tory Lemar Turner and Misti Monette Turner

Son Lawrence, Granddaughter Vera Hampton and Mildred Hampton-Henry

Family Reunion 1991

Imani Ross, Pamela Hampton Ross,
Charles Ross

Mildred Dalton Hampton Henry, Joyce
Hampton, Lawrence Hampton, Vhaness
Dalton Henderson, Glen Laque Dalton

Pamela Hampton Ross, Delano Hampton, Mildred Dalton Hampton-Henry,
Alvia Hampton Turner-Page, Lawrence Hampton

With Tribal Chief Kofi Addo in Ghana, West Africa, at a presentation from San Bernardino County. A library was named in honor of his sister. Chief Addo came to America on a steamboat to seek an education and enrolled at AM&N College in Pine Bluff, AR.

Chief Kofi Addo of Ghana, West Africa, my former school mate at AM&N College in Pine Bluff, AR, participated in graduation ceremonies at the PAL Center in San Bernardino, CA.

CSUSB Student, Hazel Ganther, paints the Signature Mural on the PAL Center Wall in Muscoy.

Granddaughters Auvria Hampton and Imani Ross at end of the
Underground Railroad Tour in Canada, 2006

A slave hideout that we saw on the
Underground Railroad to Freedom Trip.

Velma Dalton Gilbert and Milton Carl Henderson with 6-foot
ditch dug to preserve boundary of farm

Four generations of family members celebrate receiving Ph.D. at Southern Illinois University Carbondale, Illinois: Tory Turner, Lawrence Hampton, Mother Alma Dalton Gates, Joyce Hampton, Dr. Mildred Dalton Hampton-Henry, Pamela Hampton, Timetra Hampton and Mizz Turner

Alvia wears her grandmother's coat in Washington, DC with 2 million people at the Inauguration of President Barack Obama in 2009.

I also wore the coat at the Inauguration of President Bill Clinton in 1993.

Three sisters Vhaness, Velma, and Mildred in Jamaica on vacation.

Generations

Dr. Arthur Fletcher, "Father of Affirmative Action", is the Commencement speaker at PAL Center Graduation, 1995

PAL Charter Academy Graduation 2000

California State Assemblymember Jerry Eaves is Commencement Speaker

PAL Charter Academy Graduation 2014

Graduation Day

Dr. Albert Karnig, California State University San Bernardino President, speaks to PAL Center graduates, 1998 and 2010.

PAL Charter Academy/Operation Retain

Operation Safe Harbor

WIA Youth Program

Computer Institute

Supplemental Education Services

Operation Outreach

Upward Bound

PAL Comprehensive Child Care Center

PAL COMPREHENSIVE CHILD CARE CENTER & PRE-SCHOOL

A State Licensed facility, located at 1686 W. 19th Street, our child care ce
pre-school is for preschoolers aged 2-5, and school aged children aged 6
focus is on learning, tutoring, sharing, self-esteem and chronological develop

Operated in accordance with U.S. Department of Agriculture policy, which
discrimination on the basis of race, color, sex, age, handicap, religion, or
origin, the PAL Center Child Care and Pre-School is an extension of the ed
services we provide to address the growing need for more child care faciliti
community.

The center is open Monday - Friday from 6:00 a.m. to 6:00 p.m.
(Except major holidays).

Tel. (909) 887 3975

Dr. Al Karnig, President
California State University San Bernardino
at PAL Child Care Center

Dr. Al Karnig reads to children at the PAL Child Care Center

Leaving handprints in the sidewalk at the PAL Center in Muscoy, California

Sisters Vhaness and Mildred hold produce from PAL Center Gardens

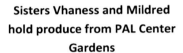

Students are taught gardening skills.

Dr. Henry and Dwaine Radden Sr. at PAL Christmas dinner

PAL Center:
Education Community Style

PAL CENTER STUDENT receives GED from Dr. Mildred Henry.
Photo: Hooks

Dr. Mildred Henry Receives International/State Honors

PAL Center Graduates 105 Students

PAL Center proud of graduates

Pathfinders for Black History Month

Public Enterprise Center is Controversial Choice

PAL Center Looking For New Home

Thursday, January 26, 1995

Inland Empire Community Achievers
Dr. Mildred D. Henry: Doing It Her Way

Groundbreaking for Dr. Mildred Dalton Henry Elementary School San Bernardino, California 2012

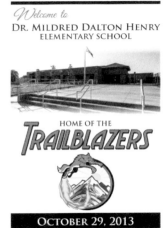

Presentation at Henry Elementary School with Principal Dr. Marcus Funchess

Sister and brother, Dr. Mildred Dalton Henry and Dr. Ulysses Grant Dalton III display Ph.D. academic regalia from Southern Illinois University Carbondale and the University of Michigan.

Nominated by Assemblymember Jerry Eaves and honored as Woman of the Year by the California State Legislature. 1991

Internationally honored entrepreneur, Dr. Joe Louis Dudley, and motivational speaker John Raye, at a banquet honoring Dr. Henry in San Bernardino.

Elected to the National Alumni Hall of Fame for the University of Arkansas at Pine Bluff. Shown here with UAPB President, Dr. Laurence Alexander.

"Taking a Knee" during the Star-Spangled Banner to support the protest against inequality in America.

California State University San Bernardino Retirement Photo with daughter-in-law Joyce, son Delano, granddaughters Auvria and Timetra, and son Lawrence Hampton

In West Africa I stood at "The Door of No Return" where slaves
were loaded on vessels and shipped across the ocean.
A very humbling experience.

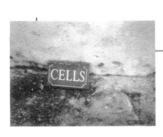

Panning for gold in Alaska

Singing the Star-Spangled Banner
at the San Bernardino
66ers Baseball game.

A sample of headlines of the numerous articles written in various newspapers about the PAL Center

Dr. Mildred Henry: Woman of Distinction

Center for students an 'oasis of hope'

By Michel Nolan
Staff Writer

It's business as usual at the PAL Center in Muscoy.

GRAND MARSHALL
"Phenomenal Woman"
DR. MILDRED DALTON HENRY
PAL Center & PAL Charter Academy
(909)887-7002
www.palcenter.org

Educator Recognized for Contributions

By Dianne Anderson
Staff Writer

ED MAUEL

My friend Millie retires in style, hers

These 10 made life a little better

A PAL IN DEEDS

Teacher Mildred Henry never gives up on kids,

The 'publish or perish' syndrome discounts professor contributions

Dr. Henry Expands PAL Ctr Services

Education

PAL Center Expands Diploma and GED Program

PART II –
THE WESTWARD TREK

XVIII

ROAD TO CALIFORNIA

Journey with me through a summative "bird's eye view" of this survivor rising from the ashes of the farm in Arkansas. I earned a Bachelor of Science degree, at age 38, from AM&N College in Pine Bluff, Arkansas in 1971, and taught music at Southeast Junior High School in Pine Bluff. This was followed by a Master's degree in Educational Counseling from Southern Illinois University, Edwardsville in 1976, and subsequent employment as the counselor at Coleman Middle School, the first middle school counselor in the Watson Chapel, Arkansas School District.

I received a Ph.D. from Southern Illinois University Carbondale in 1983, was immediately hired as Assistant Professor at California State University San Bernardino, packed my automobile, and with my son at the wheel, headed west.

At California State University San Bernardino (CSUSB), I was the first African American tenure track female professor in the School of Education. My tenure track position had been filled by an African American male who was not granted tenure after six years of employment. In fact, when I was interviewed at Lambert Airport in St. Louis, Missouri. by Dean Ernie Garcia, I inquired about the percentage of African Americans on campus. I was shown information about Professor Althea Waites in the music department. However, when I arrived, she, too, was not tenured and was no longer on faculty. The atmosphere was not conducive for the success of African American faculty, however, I decided that I WOULD be successful, WOULD get tenured, and WOULD leave the campus at **MY** determination. It was not easy, but a priority for me. I was the first African American to be tenured in the School of Education at CSUSB.

The year 1983 was monumental. I graduated with a Ph.D., my daughter Pam received her Bachelor's degree from Texas Woman's University, and her fiancé, Charles Ross, received his Bachelor's degree from Northeast Louisiana University. They were married in Pine Bluff, Arkansas one month following his graduation, and they moved immediately to Oklahoma City to enter Central State University to work on their Master's degrees.

I was interviewed and accepted a faculty position at California State University in San Bernardino, interviewed at Lambert Airport in St. Louis, Missouri, and was hired by the School of Education Dean, Dr. Ernest Garcia. I moved to California in August 1983, driven by my son, Lawrence, in our new, fully packed, Renault automobile. Pam and Charles had their first mother-in-law visit one month after their wedding as Lawrence and I drove through Oklahoma City enroute to California to begin my position as Assistant Professor in the School of Education. As we arrived at Pam and Charles' second-floor apartment, I was happy to see them safely settled. Pam had driven the moving truck from Pine

Bluff to Oklahoma City because she was the only one who could drive a stick shift, having learned with our 1951 Ford when we lived in Minnesota. She had also helped move the furniture to the second-floor apartment, displaying her "let's get it done" work ethic. We spent the night in Oklahoma and the next morning it was "California here I come!" Angels were watching over me because I found that I may not have been able to take that trip alone.

In August 1983, we arrived in San Bernardino at the Oak Tree Motel on Fifth and G Street. Without an apartment to move into, we drove to the home of Bernard and Annette Coates in the City of Rialto. They kept my belongings for one week until I found an apartment in Fontana. Bernard is the brother of Pine Bluff resident Carolyn (Wealthy) Coates.

Having accepted the position in California and knowing absolutely no one in the San Bernardino area, I contacted a former Merrill School classmate, Thomas (Tom) Stevens, who was President of Los Angeles Trade Technical College. Mr. Stevens put me in touch with Lois Carson, a prominent well-connected activist in the San Bernardino area. One of the organizers of the local chapter of the National Council of Negro Women (NCNW) organization, Mrs. Carson announced at an NCNW meeting that I was in town and needed a place to stay. Mrs. Louise Ansley immediately responded to the call. After a rather extensive search, which had begun in Carbondale, Illinois, I found an apartment at 15667 Curtis Avenue in Fontana.

The owners, Amos and Louise Ansley, lived at 6106 Knox Ave., one of the very few stone houses in the Fontana and San Bernardino areas.

Lawrence and I tried to find the Curtis Avenue location in Fontana on Friday evening, but we were unable to do so because of the impending evening darkness and unfamiliarity with the area. Lawrence boarded the train returning to Arkansas on Saturday. Sunday morning, I looked in the telephone book for an African Methodist Episcopal (AME) Church to attend. This would also identify an African American community, so I thought, I went in the wrong direction and returned to the hotel never finding the church. However, later I found and joined St. Paul AME Church in San Bernardino. Sunday afternoon I found Mrs. Louise Ansley in Fontana, saw the apartment which they furnished for me, and on Monday, I moved to 15667 Curtis Avenue in Fontana. Amos and Louise Ansley were my landlords for five years until I purchased a home and moved to Oak Hills, California in 1988. Mr. Ansley had the practice of dipping snuff and spitting into a container, however, they were sufficiently affluent to travel extensively and take cruises, carrying his snuff with them.

On Monday, I moved into the apartment and on Tuesday, Ms. Belva Holder arrived to drive Mr. and Mrs. Ansley to Newport Beach. I was invited to go on my first excursion to the beach and the ocean. A bonding friendship was formed with Belva, and it was at her home in San Bernardino that I picked fruit from the backyard and shared my desire to open an educational center. She told me of a building that she owned that could be used to actualize my dream.

XIX

THE CALIFORNIA EXPERIENCE

The California experience turned out to be quite an adventure. Santa Ana Winds are well known in California. My first encounter with the Santa Ana winds was scary. Inside my apartment in Fontana, I heard the very strong winds. Running outside to see from whence the storm was coming, I saw a blue sky. Unbelievable! What is going on? It was then that I sought information and was told about the Santa Ana winds. I was a product of the South where winds of that magnitude always indicated an approaching storm. One very unpleasant effect of the wind was the odor from a nearby chicken farm. The odorous chickens were subsequently moved, and the farm closed after about two years of my residency. The City of Fontana, I found later was famous for high winds.

As a professor at California State University, I had many students in my classes who had never had an African American professor, consequently, the first thought for many was to question my qualifications. I needed to prove that it was not the color of one's skin but rather the skill that qualifies one for employment. Students of color were limited in my classes throughout my 15-year CSUSB tenure. I may have two to three African American students in my class if any.

There was an adjustment to be made between my cultural upbringing and the laid-back California style. I wrote on the board that I was Dr. Mildred Henry and requested to be addressed in that manner. I addressed all my students with the title Mr. or Ms. unless they indicated a preference otherwise. My students varied from high school graduates to professionals working in the school districts with various career fields and varying backgrounds.

One particular student I found most interesting was Daniel Igbokwe, a Nigerian student who was paralyzed from the neck down. A Nigerian chief in his country, Mr. Igbokwe came to America to attend medical school. However, an automobile accident left him a quadriplegic who manipulated his wheelchair with his chin, and who never missed a class. Rather than be discouraged because of his accident, Daniel was not deterred and changed his career field to education. Mr. Igbokwe was an excellent mathematician and was hired at the PAL Center as a very efficient math teacher until his return to Nigeria. His male attendant was Lennox Crosby, who assisted Mr. Igbokwe inside and outside of the classroom. The students respected Mr. Igbokwe and his tenure was very effective as this gentleman modeled the determination to achieve despite adversities.

CSUSB Assistant Professor was the title of my new position in California. Nestled on 430 acres at the foot of the San Bernardino Mountains, CSUSB has an enrollment of over 20,000 students and is one of 23 California State

University campuses. I was employed in the Department of Educational Psychology and Counseling in the School of Education, later to be called the College of Education. I taught Introduction to Counseling, Multi-Cultural Counseling, Fieldwork, and other courses as assigned.

A Whale of a Tale was my first adventure in the Pacific Ocean and sailing on the water when Dr. Peggy Atwell, Professor in the School of Education, and Chair of the Department of Advanced Studies, invited me to go on a whale-watching trip. I had no idea what this entailed but I appreciated and accepted the invitation. We boarded the boat at San Pedro and sailed out into the waters. We were successful in the hunt, observed whales in the water, and the excitement and experience of my first whale encounter was most rewarding.

Dr. Atwell was instrumental in guiding me through the Faculty Activity Report (FAR) at the University. In order to be promoted, faculty members had to present written documentation of every professional activity in which they engaged, proving they had been active and competent in such fields as research and publication, professional growth, teaching, and community service. A committee judged each faculty member on these documented criteria. This FAR Report determined whether or not one would be promoted at CSUSB.

This activity was contrary to my cultural upbringing in the South. As an African American youth, I was always told that people should not brag about themselves, and to "never toot your own horn." However, this is exactly what one had to do in order to survive and justify promotion and advancement through the California State University faculty system. We learned to document every speech made, every conference attended, and every achievement, in order to qualify and prove competency in these various areas. I did not expect a thank you letter for services rendered, but this is exactly what was needed for the faculty activity report. This was definitely contrary to my upbringing.

Because of my experiences, and the uniqueness of my tenure as the first African American tenured in the School of Education, I was in demand as a speaker. I never thought of charging for speaking engagements, which I later found many of my colleagues were doing. In my culture and background, one was to give and share talents without thought of personal gain. My speaking engagements were all free, for which I have numerous plaques and recognitions. I later learned that some of my colleagues were getting paid for presenting workshops in various communities. In fact, one of my colleagues and a former student used my cross-cultural counseling materials when she was paid to train San Bernardino City Unified School District personnel in cultural workshops. It never crossed my mind to be paid for workshops, training, or speaking engagements. Another frequent saying uttered by my mother was "live and learn."

Culture Test

My training at Southern Illinois University Carbondale (SIUC) prepared me for employment as an Adjunct Professor for SIUC at the San Diego, California Naval Base on weekends. I walked into a room full of White male military personnel and wrote on the board "Dr. Mildred Henry." I said this was how I wish to be addressed and I would address them with titles, likewise. One serviceman asked, "May we call you by your first name?" I replied, "I am not sure if we have a communication problem, but I speak in English, the language is very clear, and I have indicated how I wish to be addressed." I had no further problems.

Flip Wilson, the famous comedian, had a signature statement "YOU DON'T KNOW ME THAT WELL." In the South, titles were not used with African Americans as an act of disrespect. Titles were used with "Whites Only," and not with Negroes or African Americans. Even White children were called Ms. or Mr., however, adult African Americans, regardless of age, were called by their first name. Consequently, in my cultural environment, to call an adult by the first name was disrespectful. Familiarity had to be granted. Consequently, I expect to be addressed with a title: Dr. Henry, Ms. Henry, Dr. Mildred, or a title of some kind. Exceptions are family, friends, and when permission has been granted.

After teaching every night at CSUSB, and operating the PAL Center during daytime hours, the trip to San Diego was challenging. I also accepted an adjunct professor assignment at March Air Force Base, Riverside, California which was closer. It also proved to be too demanding. However, it was in San Diego that I met the legendary Native American personality, Mr. Russell Means, of the American Indian Movement (AIM). Mr. Means was one of the leaders when Native Americans commandeered the town of Wounded Knee for two weeks in 1974.

I was eating Friday evening dinner at the hotel restaurant when a very stately Native American gentleman walked in with his wife and child. After dinner, I could not contain myself, walked over, introduced myself, and asked if he would possibly consider speaking to my classes. He replied that he would love to except he was not from the area. To my chagrin, I found that he was in town to attend a Pow Wow the next day at CSUSB. When he gave me his card, I was absolutely stunned at having the opportunity to meet this renowned individual. Needless to say, I attended the Pow Wow the next day. This was my first experience with this wonderful display of Native American culture. What an experience!

Fight for the Right

In order to be promoted from Assistant Professor to Associate Professor, I had to document volumes of work and activities and appear before an evaluation committee to be judged by my colleagues. The promotion from Assistant to Associate went smoothly with no problems. The advancement to Full Professor was a different story.

The major discrepancy was in the classification of community service. My major community involvement was organizing the PAL Center, a community-based 501(c)(3) education and vocational center.

The PAL Center was organized in 1984 and during the day I worked at the PAL Center from 8:00 A.M. to approximately 3:30 P.M. CSUSB office hours began at 4 P.M., and my evening classes were from 6 P.M. to 10 P.M. This was a daily routine. When I applied for full professor, the School Committee denied my recommendation for promotion, citing a lack of professional growth. I felt a personal affront, knowing there were personality issues involved. A professor that I introduced into the community, who later became Chairman of The Department of Advanced Studies, was instrumental in the denial. We brought the professor on board at the PAL Center as a member of The Provisional Educational Services, Inc. Board of Directors. However, there were compatibility issues, and his membership was discontinued. Thinking some personal conflicts were involved in the promotion denial, I was determined to secure the title of Full Professor, and I began activities to claim my rightful place in the order. This bump in the road would not deter my journey to success! The fight was on!

I had volumes of documents validating workshops, conferences, speaking engagements, publications, newspaper articles, everything needed to document that the necessary activities for promotion had been performed. The committee cited a lack of professional growth as the area insufficiently attained. Conversely, I thought this was my strongest area. I had founded and established an entire educational system in the community that provided tutoring, high school diplomas, GEDs, youth employment training and employment, and other services. However, my work was not completely ignored at CSUSB. In September 1994, a letter from Dr. J. C. Robinson granted me a "0.50 leave without pay to operate the Provisional Accelerated Learning (PAL) Center."

Still ringing in my ears were the words of the White realtor who told my mother, "Your little nigger kids ain't never gonn' 'mount to nothing nohow." Our Black teachers told us, "You must be 'better than' in order to prove your worth." I determined to win the title of full professor that I had rightfully earned.

With my documentation in hand, I went to organizations such as the Westside Action Group (WAG), wrote newspaper articles, and made known my perceptions of inequity on the campus. I researched statistics and wrote an article, "WILL THE REAL CSUSB PLEASE STAND UP?" which was published in the community newspapers. This infuriated the CSUSB President, however, the data was documented, accurate, and could not be refuted. The title of the article was patterned after a popular TV show and the article revealed research on the inequitable employment and status of minorities at CSUSB. The data was presented and "figures do not lie." CSUSB President Dr. Anthony Evans told me they "could not give" me anything, to which I replied, "I don't want anything given to me, however, I intend to get what I earned." I also told the School of Education faculty in a meeting, that I would get promoted to full professor and I would "not kiss anyone's backside" to get it. To quote the proverbial statement, "You could hear a pin drop on the carpet."

Upon arrival at CSUSB, I was told that I should not concentrate on the community but instead stay on campus and teach and research in order to get promoted. However, there were predecessors to whom I owed a debt, and the need for dropout prevention was so great in the community that I set up an entire educational system to help alleviate the problem.

Most people were aware of my dispute with CSUSB. I had the support of The Black Faculty and Staff Association on campus. In fact, at one time, I was PRESIDENT of the Black Faculty and Staff Association. I was a member of the California Faculty Association (CFA) and met with them to discuss my dilemma and enlist their aid. They sent a representative to campus and when I saw him, "my feathers fell." I thought that surely this Ivy League, pinstripe-suited, preppy-looking gentleman would never understand the importance of community-based education and services primarily designed for lesser advantaged populations. However, this gentleman proved me wrong.

Meanwhile, I had recruited Dr. Carolyn Murray, a well-known professor at the University of California, Riverside, to meet with the CFA representative. Dr. Murray is a recognized expert and had done extensive research on the education of Blacks, disadvantaged populations, and related societal issues. Dr. Murray was recruited to validate the importance of community-based education. She discussed her research and greatly impressed the CFA representative.

Following her presentation and the documentation that I presented, the CFA representative ruled in my favor. Saying that he could not overturn the decision, however, he requested that my file be re-evaluated, and he would retain jurisdiction over the process until the matter was resolved. The old adage came to mind, "never judge a book by its cover." He understood and I won the case. Subsequently, I received a letter from CSUSB Vice President Louis Fernandez stating, "In compliance with an arbitration decision dated August 22, 1995, the University offers you a promotion to the rank of Professor, retroactive to September 1, 1993." I fought that battle for two years.

Many times, during the battle, discouragement tried to rear its ugly head but was rebuffed. These are the times when we pull on the spiritual resources embedded through the years. I could hear mother get up in the morning singing hymns and Negro spirituals.

"I woke up this morning with my mind
stayed on Jesus,

*I woke up this morning with my mind
stayed on Jesus.*

*I woke up this morning with my mind
stayed on Jesus. Hallelu, Hallelu,
Hallelujah."*

This spirited song of hope erased any doubts as to the direction I should take. I had the total support of the Black Faculty and Staff Association at CSUSB, however, some individuals in the community were seemingly unaware of the racial climate at the University, and the disparities that existed, and they supported the administration in the dispute. All they had to do was count the numbers, and to this way of thinking we applied the African proverb, "ONE WHO IS BEING CARRIED DOES NOT REALIZE HOW FAR THE TOWN."

The cultural diversity climate was not the best at CSUSB. The professor that I replaced, Dr. Persons, was not tenured after six years of service. I had the pleasure of meeting Dr. Persons in 2015 and found him to be a dedicated and possibly too-militant personality for CSUSB at the time of his employment. I determined that no one would run me away from that University. I vowed to obtain tenure, the necessary promotions, and leave when I was ready to go. This I owed to all of my predecessors who paved the way. Gratefully, I was able to fulfill that promise, and I retired from CSUSB in June 1995 as a Full Professor. I was also awarded the title of Professor

Emeritus by CSUSB's newly appointed President Dr. Albert Karnig.

A favorite poem from Bowles Book of Poetry states:

If you think you are whipped, You are whipped;

If you think you've won, You've won;

For you never are whipped 'Till your wings are clipped,

And you never are done 'Till you've won.

Mission Accomplished to the glory of my predecessors, and The Legacy Continues!

XX

STONY THE ROAD

"No MAN IS AN ISLAND; NO MAN STANDS ALONE" are words that I sang many times in choral groups that motivated and influenced my life codes. I was motivated to fight for my rights in California by warriors in my past. My California experiences are rooted in the Delta sands of Arkansas. Pine Bluff was a cultural and historical Mecca and the original center of Arkansas' African American influence. Legendary African Americans from this region have contributed in all fields of endeavor, including agriculture, politics, music, technology, education, medicine, literature, business, science, art, civil rights, and numerous other areas of civilized society. The renowned Mr. Booker T. Washington in his book, <u>THE NEGRO IN BUSINESS</u>, states, "In the course of my journey through Arkansas and the Territories, I made the acquaintance of no community where it seemed to me to have more real progress than that of Pine Bluff."

It is this environment and training in Arkansas that prepared me for the California experience. This background also shaped the character of numerous individuals who have made history throughout the world. A prevalent mistaken belief is that southern African Americans were poor and disenfranchised. However, in the 1900's at least four Pine Bluff residents were millionaires when equated to today's market value. There are also families that have been well-known for achieving firsts, i.e., the ULYSSES GRANT DALTON *Family of Tamo,* who owned the first cotton gin and general store in Southeast Arkansas owned by African Americans.

The Harold Flowers Family members are well-known pioneers in politics and medicine. The Wiley Branton, Sr. and Cleon Flowers families of lawyers and doctors are among others who achieved national recognition. Wiley Branton, Sr. was a successful co-counsel in the Central High School Little Rock Nine Crisis of 1957. His brother, Leo Branton, successfully defended militant activist Angela Davis. Other Pine Bluffians were quite prominent in the desegregation of Central High School. In addition to Wiley Branton, Sr. working with Attorney Thurgood Marshall, the Dalton Family's lawyer, Attorney George Howard, whose daughter attended Central High School, was also a member of that legal team.

Single-parent mother of five, MRS. EDNA MAYS, parented three medical doctors, a librarian, and a career military serviceman. The McKissics, The Kearneys were also families of prominent achievement. The list goes on and on. Several noteworthy institutions provided education for these prominent citizens.

Branch Normal College, established in 1873, attended by my mother, was an icon that was educationally comparative to California. The first Principal was Joseph Carter Corbin, a profound mathematician, a talented musician, and a linguist who read and spoke Latin,

German, French, Spanish, Hebrew, and Danish. He was the eldest of 11 children born to former slave parents.

In 1895, the women's dormitory had a capacity of 35 residents. The cost was $2 per week paid in advance. Branch Normal subsequently became Agricultural, Mechanical, and Normal College (AM&N), where all four Dalton siblings graduated. AM&N graduated renowned pioneers in numerous civic and scientific endeavors. One history-making graduate in 1952 was Dr. Samuel Kountz who, after failing the AM&N Historically Black College (HBC) entrance exam, appealed to President A. Davis, was allowed to remain in school, and went on to graduate with honors. Dr. Kountz became the first doctor in the world to perform a successful kidney transplant between a recipient and a donor who were not identical twins. At the University of California, San Francisco, he also developed the largest kidney transplant and research program in the country.

AM&N was also at the forefront of the Civil Rights Movement. When Dr. Lawrence A. Davis invited Dr. Martin Luther King to give the commencement address in 1958, angry Arkansas legislators cut the annual appropriations for the school by $50,000 for several years. When I returned to college at age 38, a single parent with four children to support, President Davis (Prexy), and Music Department Head and Choir Director, Mr. Ariel M. Lovelace ("Pops") provided me with a job to support my children and continue my education.

In 1972, AM&N College became the University of Arkansas at Pine Bluff. AM&N college was nationally known for colorful parades, featuring beautiful floats and marching bands. Participants came from numerous states, from as far away as the State of Michigan. The yearly parade up Main Street was a major event in the African American culture.

As I reflected on my road to California, I wanted to revisit stops along the journey. Our documentary team went to Pine Bluff to capture some of the rapidly diminishing culture that launched so many renowned champions into their fields of endeavor.

Merrill High School. In 1892, this 10,000 ft. public school was one of the largest buildings in Pine Bluff. Merrill was respected throughout Arkansas because of its outstanding graduates and leadership. I was amazed to learn that students were exposed to trailblazers such as Marian Anderson, Joe Louis, Mary McLeod Bethune, and Jesse Owens, to name a few. I attended the Merrill building that was constructed in 1930 and included an elementary school. The elementary school separated later and was named Carver Elementary School. At Merrill, Black history and culture was paramount. We sang the Negro National Anthem, LIFT EVERY VOICE AND SING, at every assembly. We had outstanding choirs, bands, and Merrill won the Black high school national football championships in 1933 AND 1934.

Merrill students became several historical "firsts." The Edwards-Wilkins families had the first sister and brother team, Jean and Josetta, serving simultaneously in the Arkansas State House of Representatives. Henry Wilkins III, in 1972, was one of three African Americans elected to the Arkansas legislature since Reconstruction. He was succeeded by his wife Dr. Josetta Edwards Wilkins, who was reelected and termed out. Henry Wilkins was my elementary and junior high school classmate.

Merrill High School was integrated with Pine Bluff High School in 1970. My daughter Alvia graduated with the class of 1971, the first integrated class at Pine Bluff High School. The historic Merrill High School building, which served Black students from 1886 to 1976, was torched by arsonists on July 7, 1986. All but the auditorium of the large brick building "crashed into flaming rubble at about midnight," according to the PINE BLUFF COMMERCIAL NEWSPAPER.

Jefferson County Historical Museum, which houses artifacts and history-making events that shaped the culture of the area - from cotton picking paraphernalia, to civil rights sit-ins, and marches was visited. The museum is housed in the old train station where African Americans boarded separate railway passenger cars, usually the last car. The train station was reportedly the only public place in town where Blacks could use the restroom facilities. This was especially pertinent on Saturdays when "country folks came to town" and needed accommodations. I rode this train monthly from Pine Bluff to St. Louis to obtain treatment for my feet.

<u>University of Arkansas at Pine Bluff (UAPB) Museum and Cultural Center</u> at The University of Arkansas at Pine Bluff is known as "The Flagship of the Delta." It is the second oldest public education institution in Arkansas and the oldest college with a Black heritage. The University Museum is the home of the display "KEEPERS OF THE SPIRIT," a widely acclaimed collection of Black culture that documents the lives of people who shaped the history of the University, the Delta, and the world. It has drawn rave reviews and reported as a "best museum" from such noted individuals as Nikki Giovanni and Cornell West. The museum has been featured on ESPN-TV. This museum contains some artifacts from the Dalton cotton gin, the general store, and historical memoirs of the Dalton Family achievements. U.G. Dalton III's picture is on a permanent wall display in the museum.

<u>Artistic Historian, Professor Henri Linton</u> is a retired Head of the Art Department at UAPB and was inducted into the Arkansas Black Hall of Fame in 2001. He is one of the best-known landscape artists in the State of Arkansas. Also, considered a preeminent historian, Mr. Linton organized and is the Director of the UAPB Museum. He also has an extensive worldwide collection of "first editions" of books and paraphernalia. Collections include historical items such as <u>Color Magazine</u>, the publication by Arkansas native Ira Wells, which preceded Ebony magazine. Mr.

Linton, artist extraordinaire, also has first edition coins of Booker T. Washington and other famous history makers.

AM&N/UAPB Alumni Hall of Fame has my photo on display at the National Alumni Hall of Fame in Caldwell Hall on the UAPB campus. Nominated by the Southern California Alumni Chapter, I was presented at the 2014 homecoming game. Inductees were honored on the football field at half-time ceremonies and in the Alumni Assembly.

Dr. W.E. O'Bryant Bell Tower, completed in 1947, is an iconic symbolic emblem for the AM&N/UAPB Family. The structure was built over a four-year period by students and faculty from private donations. The campus centralized Bell Tower is the site for campus assemblies, music concerts, rallies, and other significant events. Dr. O'Bryant was a pharmacist who owned a drugstore and was a member of St. John AME Church. "Lady" O'Bryant was a public-school teacher and was my Sunday School primary grade teacher at St. John AME Church.

Pine Bluff Downtown Murals has artistic displays of historical and noted African American history and individuals displayed on the walls of downtown buildings. One mural depicts four college presidents, Doctors J.C. Corbin, John Watson, Lawrence A. Davis, and Isaac Fisher, along with the Agricultural, Mechanical, and Normal (Teacher's) College themes. The walls depict the historical progress of Pine Bluff and its prominence.

The Masonic Temple, a four-story building that was constructed in 1904, at a cost of $50,000, the modern equivalent of today's $1.3 million, was the largest building in Pine Bluff. Over the years the building contained offices for many of Pine Bluff's African American professionals. My general medicine practitioner, my dentist, my attorney, and other professionals were all housed in that building.

Main Street Pine Bluff, until recent years, hosted the college and university homecoming parades, which was the "Black Culture on Parade" event of the year. The Jefferson County Courthouse at the end of Main Street was a symbolic focal point where the parade ended. Sit-ins and protests were held at places like the "Kress 5 & 10 Cents Store," but the parades held on Main Street were unifying events. Daughter Pamela was a majorette for Carver Elementary School in the parade. In 2016, the majority of the parade was not held on Main Street. The courthouse was not the symbolic structure at the end of the parade that it had been for decades. The railroad tracks crossing Main Street did not interrupt the parade. It was hurtful to see so many businesses boarded up and buildings tumbled into the streets. Main Street has fallen prey to the lure of businesses in outlying areas.

St. John AME Church was my home church from approximately 1942 to 1980. St. John Church members taught, trained, and prepared professionals that achieved international recognition. I learned to read the Sunday School primary cards sitting around a table and taught by

Lady O'Bryant, wife of pharmacist, Dr. William O'Bryant. My spiritual home since about third grade, I worshipped in the building that was constructed in 1897 and replaced in 1966. The Church members, participants, teachers, and church leaders were also professionals and leaders in the community. We had many role models to emulate.

121 N. Oak Street was the site of the first house purchased by Mom and Dad "in town" so that their four children could get a nine-month education. The White neighbor next door, across the alley at 123 N. Oak, infuriated Mother by saying we "looked like decent people." Mother was a schoolteacher, musician, and prominent citizen in the community. To be told such was an insult. One of my responsibilities which I enjoyed was to keep the grounds looking good, cutting the grass, trimming the hedges, etc. Ironically, my children and I briefly lived at 123 N. Oak Street when we moved to Pine Bluff in 1969. When the freeway was built, it demolished part of the 121 N. Oak Street house site. The freeway also destroyed the historic home of Miss Myrtle Jones, one block away. Miss Jones was an educational and probation department icon in the community.

Southeast Junior High School was my first full-time teaching position as a music teacher after obtaining my Bachelor's degree in music. Lawrence played the baritone horn in the school band under Mr. Maurice Carlton. I attended Merrill High School and taught at Southeast Jr. High School. Consequently, I carried the banner and represented both schools in alumni homecoming parades.

<u>Carver Elementary School</u> was where my two youngest children, Pamela and Lawrence, attended school when I returned to Arkansas from Minnesota. Pam was a majorette. Daughter Alvia and son Delano were next door at Merrill High School. Alvia played tenor saxophone and flute, and Del played bass clarinet in the high school band. Alvia was in the band and the high school orchestra. Pam also later played the tenor saxophone, in Pine Bluff and at Normandy High School in St. Louis, Missouri.

Several houses paid a prominent role along the stony road to success.

<u>Our McFadden Road </u>home was built shortly after my marriage in 1972 to Rev. Hayward Henry, pastor of Faith Presbyterian Church in Pine Bluff. McFadden Road is where we lived and worked when all of the children and I completed high school, college, and graduate schools. We lived on McFadden Road when I earned both my Master's and Doctorate degrees at Southern Illinois University. While attending Southern Illinois University in Carbondale, I taught at the Parish Elementary School, Carbondale School District. When we lived on McFadden Road, my son, Lawrence, at age 13, rode his bicycle approximately 16 miles per trip into Pine Bluff in order to work at Meadors Service Station.

<u>Pine Bluff Arsenal</u>, established in 1941, produced incendiary munitions, stockpiled chemical warfare agents, and experimented with germ warfare. Mother performed clerical work at the Arsenal during the war years. The

McFadden Road house is across the road from the Arsenal.

<u>Main Street Dalton Home</u>, the Oak Street Dalton house that was moved from 121 Oak Street to 3522 Main Street, was reportedly torched by an arsonist. A bigger and better house was built by my brother who purchased the original Oak Street house. This was a beautiful "stop-by" home for visiting family. As the oldest of the siblings, my brother's family was something of an umbrella. Sister-in-law Helen Louise, an elementary school teacher, was a mother to all children.

<u>The Victorian-style house of Velma Dalton Gilbert</u> should be on the historic register as are some of the surrounding houses owned by White individuals. This house, and several nearby houses owned by African Americans, were never approved for the funding and renovation. My sister's house was also home to family members when in town. My daughter, Pam, stayed with Velma the year I was away earning my doctorate.

XXX

THE FARM

It was the Dalton Farm at Tamo that propelled me to California. I was born and grew up on those revered lands. Cotton was the predominant crop when I was a child. Today, few cotton fields exist. Mostly corn, soybeans, and rice crops are harvested. In 2016, when we retraced our footsteps, rice was being grown and harvested on the Dalton farm and we watched our African American renter harvesting the rice fields with his huge combines. My daughter, Alvia, and I were fascinated by picking rice from the field. This was a joyful sight! Expensive machinery has forced many small farmers out of business and replaced human field workers.

The approximate 211-acre Dalton farm was purchased in parcels, such as the "80-acre Washington tract." The Dalton farm consists of approximately "127 acres West of Highway 65 South, 34 acres East of Highway 65, and 50 acres on Long Lake." We dug a 6-foot ditch on the Long Lake property because White neighbors repeatedly encroached on our property, necessitating our going to court several times to prove ownership.

Portions of the Washington Tract were divided into lots and a subdivision is still on record at the Jefferson County Courthouse as the "TOWN OF DALTON." The town, however, did not materialize. The dream was killed with the burning of the farm. The idea of the town was desecrated, but the spirit of entrepreneurship rose from those ashes and spread, as far as San Bernardino, California.

This is the background that forged the path for my California sojourn.

XXII

BIRTH OF A DREAM

Upon receiving my Ph.D. in Counseling and Educational Psychology, I searched the Chronicle of Higher Education for a job, applied, was interviewed, and accepted a position of Counselor Educator at California State University San Bernardino. The idea of becoming a counselor was the result of the loss of our oldest child, my son Angelo Jerome. Unable to recognize the signs of his pending suicide, I decided on a career in counseling. I was unable to save my son but felt I may save others.

Upon arriving in San Bernardino and working at California State University, I felt the need "to pay some dues." At a National Association for the Advancement of Colored People (NAACP) meeting in San Bernardino. I asked about the needs of the community, and what I could do in the area. Maurice Roberson told me to look at the dropout rate, particularly among African American youth. I did so, and it became a determining factor for my community involvement. I saw children dropping out of school, babies having babies, children getting high on alcohol and drugs, and I felt the need to do something about the problems. Booker T. Washington said, "Put down your bucket where you are." I did.

In 1984, the dream and concept for Provisional Educational Services Incorporated and the Provisional

Accelerated Learning (PAL) Center was organized and actualized in a house at 15667 Curtis Avenue, in Fontana, California. This dreamer made several trips to Los Angeles to visit Arkansas classmate, Doretha McCoy Webster, and husband John Webster, who owned a daycare center on Crenshaw Boulevard. I shared my dream, observed their operation, and discussed incorporating a business. The papers were drawn up by John Webster.

John, a Notary Public, flew to Sacramento with incorporation papers in order to expedite the process. The chosen and preferred name was Diversified Services Incorporated. However, that name was already taken, and John Webster, on the spot, chose the name Provisional Educational Services, in order to get the incorporation process completed while in Sacramento. He came back with the Incorporated name in December 1984. I put the dream on paper while working as a full-time Assistant Professor in the School of Education at California State University San Bernardino.

In 1985, the proposal was written for Operation RETAIN (Rescue Educational Training and Initiative Now). Never having written a proposal before, I consulted with Messrs. Alonzo Thompson, and Alvin Ricks, a Field Representative for Assemblyman Jerry Eaves of Rialto, CA. With their suggestions for modifications, the first vocational training proposal was funded by Delores Carter, Director of the San Bernardino County Job Training and Employment Resources Agency. She gave the proposal to employee Beverly Wilson to see if it could be funded. With modifications, the first successful Provisional Educational Services, Incorporated vocational training program was funded.

The dream was shared with Belva holder, and the facility at 1686 W. 19th St. in San Bernardino, the former Mother Goose Nursery, was obtained from Mrs. Holder. Belva donated the facility for months because there was no available rental money. The PAL Center doors opened on January 5, 1985, with one teacher, Randall Slotkin, and one student. Dr. Mildred Henry was Director; Mr. Alonzo Thompson, Assistant Director; Mr. Roger Mulligan, Coordinator; and Ms. Patricia Butler was the Secretary. Since that time Provisional Educational Services and The PAL Center have continuously provided community-based services to hundreds of thousands of individuals in the Inland Empire and beyond.

Programs that provided services over the years were numerous. The first funded program in 1985, <u>PROJECT EARN AND LEARN</u>, a summer youth employment program, was funded by the San Bernardino City Private Industry Council. <u>OPERATION RETAIN</u> (Rescue Educational Training and Initiative Now), was founded in 1985 by the San Bernardino County Private Industry Council, later to be named the San Bernardino County Jobs and Employment Services (JESD). They continuously funded our programs over the years. The names of programs have changed but the mission has remained the same - providing employment and employment training for youth and adults. The dream which was conceptualized at "The Duck

Inn", a college hangout located near Agricultural, Mechanical, and Normal (AM&N) College, a Historically Black College, in Pine Bluff, Arkansas, was to become a reality near a college in San Bernardino, California.

It was upon arriving in San Bernardino on August 31, 1983, for employment as an Assistant Professor at California State University San Bernardino, that the dream was put into the process. In October 1983, I attended an NAACP conference in San Bernardino. We discussed the needs of the community, and I began to solicit the first board members for a community-based nonprofit organization. The first board members were Mildred Henry, President; Belva Holder, Secretary; Maurice Roberson, Treasurer; and Alonzo Thompson, Dr. Margaret Cooney, Dr. Melvin Hawkins, and Kathy Holder.

Board members over the years have included such personalities as Ms. Dorothy Ingram, Retired Superintendent of Schools, and numerous other titles; Stephen Whitney, San Bernardino City Librarian; Dr. Robert Detweiler, President of California State University Dominguez Hills; Dr. Sidney Ribeau, President of Ohio State University at Bowling Green, Ohio, as well as President of Howard University in Washington, D.C.; Eugene Woods, Vice President and Manager of Security Pacific National Bank; Dr. Lamar Foster, Pastor New Hope Baptist Church; Rev. Charles Brooks, Pastor, St. Paul AME Church; Raul Mercado, Owner, All American Auto Parts; James Busby, TRW Administrator and former Mayor of the City of Victorville; Linvol Henry, CPA and Professor in

Accounting and Finance, Cal State University; Dr. Victor Edinburg, Principal of San Andreas High School; Dr. Aubrey Bonnet, Dean California State University San Bernardino; John Dukes, Community Developer; and other community leaders. Long-term board members include Robert Jenkins (1986), Georgia Morris (1986), Marion Black (1989), Linda Letson (1989), and Stan Charzn (1993). MR. MARION BLACK HOLDS THE RECORD FOR LONGEVITY. HE IS STILL AN ACTIVE *Provisional Educational Services, Incorporated* (PESI) BOARD MEMBER IN THE YEAR 2021. Long-term and early employees include Lawrence Hampton (1991), and Tammie Hicks (1991).

Diverse programs were added at various times. They included "TEENS FOR RESPONSIBLE BEHAVIOR"; "TRAINING INTERNSHIP AND PLACEMENT (TIP); "PROJECT EARLY OUTREACH," an elementary school tutoring program; ALTERNATIVE STREET ACADEMY, a tutorial program funded by the San Bernardino City Unified School District; "TALENT SEARCH," a U.S. Department of Education TRIO college prep program that serviced over 1000 youth each year for six years; "UPWARD BOUND" a college prep program for high school students; "OPERATION RECOVERY," adult literacy program; a childcare center; "ELECTRIC EDUCATION PROGRAM"; "OPERATION SAFE HARBOR," a homeless shelter program for youth; and "SUBSTANCE ABUSE MOBILE (SAM)," a traveling RV substance abuse and gang intervention program, which was toured and viewed by over 350,000 individuals in person and on TV. SAM visited schools, churches, street corners, college campuses, and other community events.

We have a rich heritage of service in the community and have survived many up and down funding periods. Numerous personally-financed trips were made to Washington D.C., Sacramento, California, and other areas to attend conferences, write proposals, seek funding, and network with others. All programs except Upward Bound and the Electric Education Program were written in-house.

We have graduated thousands with high school diplomas, GEDs, and English as A Second Language Certificates, and our services expanded to include a charter school, The PAL Charter Academy (PCA). Thousands of individuals have been trained and placed in employment and have been assisted in their efforts to go to college. The PAL Center was featured on Channel 2 Television and has been a major education and training facility, and employment agency in the San Bernardino area and the Inland Empire since 1985. The dream is always in process and must forever grow, expand, and be kept alive.

Provisional Educational Services, Incorporated, the PAL Center, and The PAL Charter Academy, in San Bernardino, were not successfully organized by a "little woman wearing a Superman cape," but rather by many dedicated collaborators who fertilized a seed and were determined to challenge minds and save lives. The seed was planted, but many people fertilized the seed to become the tree that changed the lives of thousands of individuals. I shared my dream of a vocational school for pregnant girls and young mothers, who stumbled but needed help to "get up and win the race," with a St. Paul AME Church member Alonzo Thompson. Mr. Thompson introduced me to Alvin Ricks who read the proposal and provided feedback. When completed, Alonzo Thompson suggested that I take the proposal to John Dukes in San Bernardino, a prominent community developer, who later became a member of the PESI Board of Directors. However, upon arrival in the parking lot, a gentleman suggested that I take the proposal to Deloris Carter at the San Bernardino County Workforce Development Department. The PAL Center was funded and has received continuous funding from different sources since 1985.

Belva Holder's building at 1686 W. 19th St. became the first PAL Center, opening with one student and one teacher. In that building, we tutored elementary and high school students. Our Project Early Outreach directed by Sharon Atkins was a most successful community venture. Students were tutored free of charge, mainly supported by CSUSB students who performed fieldwork and community service hours.

This full-time Assistant Professor at CSUSB was greatly concerned about the struggling youth in the community. I knocked on numerous doors with my proposal. Someone suggested I contact Judge Patrick Morris, who sent me to his brother-in-law at the San Bernardino City Unified School District. Ideas were circulated and possibilities were beginning to surface.

Another suggestion for possible funding was the Job Training and Partnership Act (JTPA) program in San Bernardino. It was funded by San Bernardino County, and we have continuously provided youth employment and training services to thousands of youths and adults for more than 36 years.

We continually wrote and submitted successful proposals, and provided General Education Development (GED) certificates, and High School Diplomas (HSD) through the Colton, Fontana and Snowline Unified School Districts. Snowline offered educational services through the Eagle Summit Academy High School in Phelan. The PAL Center provided education, vocational training, and work experience for youth and adults and agencies, such as The Job Corps in San Bernardino.

When we outgrew the building on 19th Street, New Hope Missionary Baptist Church provided a house on Medical Center Dr., at no cost, for one year. Lawrence Hampton joined the organization at that point, driving his family from Little Rock, Arkansas. We placed offices in that building and retained 19th Street for training purposes.

After one year we secured a building at Highland and State Streets, where all services were combined. On State Street, we added additional programs such as GREATER AVENUES TO INDEPENDENCE (GAIN) and other welfare reform programs; ADULT BASIC EDUCATION (ABE); ENGLISH AS A SECOND LANGUAGE (ESL), including

VOCATIONAL ESL; SUBSTANCE ABUSE AND GANG INTERVENTION programs; HOMELESS YOUTH transitional housing, education, and employment programs; UPWARD BOUND for college potential students; COMPUTER INSTITUTE; and other programs. The building on 19th Street became a childcare center.

We outgrew the building on State Street and Highland Avenue and were offered the Anna Hobart Park and community center in Muscoy by San Bernardino County Supervisor Jerry Eaves. Because Muscoy residents would not approve a tax increase for the upkeep of the community park, we were given possession with the except for the Little League softball field, which was occupied by another entity. There was one permanent structure, a concrete block building on the premises, which was used for the community center. Community meetings continued to be held after our occupancy.

In order to accommodate our growth, each year we applied for CDBG (Community Development Block Grant) monies to add additional buildings. We also secured San Bernardino County mobile buildings from the Gilbert Street hospital grounds. The building expansion projects were under the supervision of the San Bernardino County Special Districts Department. All projects were overseen by Supervisor Jerry Eaves' office and staff. The San Bernardino County Fifth District Supervisor, and his staff, were staunch supporters of the PAL Center, alerting us to funding possibilities.

Funding from the 12-month Workforce Investment Act (WIA) program for low-income youth, a program funded by the San Bernardino City and County Private Industry Councils, enabled the PAL Center to provide work training and employment for thousands of youths.

The PAL Center's academic component also flourished. On a trip to Sacramento for one of our programs, I met Rex Crossen, who was a key figure in California's recognized "Educational Clinics." The Educational Clinics were tantamount to being accredited at that time. Rex visited our programs in Muscoy, introduced me to the U.S. Department of Education representative in San Francisco, and the PAL Center became an SB (Senate Bill) 65 Educational Clinic.

XXIII

BENEFACTORS

Each year has been a progressive attainment. In 1992, we graduated five GED students and awarded 10 Adult Basic Education certificates. In 1999, we graduated 105 students – 72 with GEDs and 33 with high school diplomas. San Bernardino City Mayor, Judith Valles was the commencement speaker.

We have had excellent local, national, and internationally-known speakers come to the PAL Center. Graduation speakers included but were not limited to City of San Bernadino San Bernardino Mayor Judith Valles and City of Fontana Mayor Aquanetta Warren; County and State Legislators Jerry Eaves and Nell Soto; TV personality and Channel 4 Commentator, Beverly White; Los Angeles Trade-Technical College President Mr. Thomas Stevens and CSUSB President Dr. Albert Karnig; Heavyweight Boxing Champion of the World Rubin "The Hurricane" Carter; one of the original "Little Rock Nine," Dr. Terrance Roberts; Dr. Renatta Osterdock who CNN recognized for separating conjoined twins, Dr. George McKenna, who was the subject of a movie featuring Denzel Washington (The George Mckenna Story); and Dr. Arthur Fletcher the Father of Affirmative Action appointed by President Richard Nixon, just to name a few of our outstanding speakers. Strong supporter San Bernardino County

Supervisor Josie Gonzales attended our graduations, whether or not she was the keynote speaker.

In addition to graduations, we have had excellent national and internationally known speakers. For example, Mr. Joe Louis Dudley, one of the world's most sought-after entrepreneurial masterminds, owner of a multi-million-dollar hair care and cosmetic company, came to the PAL Center to share. In his autobiography, <u>WALKING BY FAITH I CAN, I AM, I WILL,</u> Mr. Dudley reveals how he was labeled retarded, retained in the first and 11th grades, suffered from a speech impediment, and his mother was told he would never be anybody. She encouraged him otherwise. He parlayed a $10 cosmetic sales kit into an over $35 million enterprise and is the owner of one of the largest cosmetic manufacturing firms in the nation. While in college, after being told by a competitor that he was retarded, he taught himself to read starting with first-grade books. He paid his way through North Carolina A&T State University selling door door-to-door products. Dr. Joe Louis Dudley was the keynote speaker at a PAL Center dinner when the California State Assembly named Dr. Mildred Henry, 1990 Woman of the Year.

Various funding agencies for PAL Center programs have included, but have not been limited to, the U.S. Department of Education, U.S. Department of Housing and Urban Development, U.S. Department of Health and Human Services, San Bernardino City Private Industry Council, San Bernardino County Private Industry Council, San Bernardino County Career Training and Development

Department, San Bernardino County Department of Job Training and Employment Resources, San Bernardino City Unified School District, San Bernardino SUN Newspaper, San Bernardino City Employment and Training Agency, Community Action Partnership, and the San Bernardino City Economic Development Agency.

California activists gave birth to the PAL Center. Community leaders and their political bosses guided me through the political process. Congressman George Brown and Wilmer Carter; Wes Jefferson, Al Twine and Assemblyman Jerry Eaves, Frank Stallworth and Senator Reuben Ayala, Ernie Wilson and Mayor "Bob" Holcomb, Keith Lee and County Supervisor Robert Hammock, Michael Townsend and Assemblyman Joe Baca, Assemblyman John Longville, Sixth Ward Councilperson Betty Anderson, San Bernardino City Mayor Evelyn Wilcox, and many others helped implement this novel, much needed, community-based program.

The dream was shared by many benefactors who made it happen. Supervisor Jerry Eaves and staff provided Community Development Block Grant monies for buildings and land. California State University students volunteered at the PAL Center. Daniel Igbokwe was hired as a most efficient math teacher. Cal State Professors Dr. Margaret Cooney, who was on the first PESI Corporate Board, and Dr. Jean Peacock, President of the CSUSB Black Faculty and Staff was also President of the PAL Charter Academy Advisory Committee; the Professors were prominent supporters.

Lawrence Hampton, my son and Chief Financial Officer, and Tammie Amis, a loyal employee with the PAL Center for over 32 years, worked with me writing grants and running to the post office at 11:30 P.M. with proposals to mail before midnight deadlines. Dr. Margaret Hill, Principal at San Andreas High School mentored our first Principal, Tom Cass. She later became President of the San Bernardino City Unified School District Board of Education. Danny Tillman fixed our older computers and Walter Hawkins also repaired computers, did research, and helped write the Talent Search Grant. Mr. Alonzo Thompson was Associate Director of the PAL Center until his demise in February 2005. The list goes on and on.

In the formative stages of the PAL Center, one of the initial strong supporters of the PAL Center and our community-based services was newspaper columnist, Ed Mauel, of the San Bernardino County SUN newspaper. Mr. Mauel wrote newspaper articles on the PAL Center so frequently that people asked if he was on the PAL Center payroll. The same was asked of Diane Anderson, of the Precinct Reporter Newspaper. The novel community-based PAL Center educational programs also had great support from other community newspapers such as the Black Voice, the Westside Story, the San Bernardino American News, and the El Chicano Newspapers.

The initial contact with Ed Mauel, newspaper columnist, was when I was presenting a workshop at California State University, and he was the adjudicator for the workshop. I did not know who he was until an article appeared in the SUN Newspaper in which he reported on my topic of education for disadvantaged students. The workshop, VOICE OF THE LOW IQ, stressed the fact that no one is dumb, and we must prevent students from dropping out of school. Mr. Mauel also relates how he came to the PAL Center looking for Dr. Henry, and upon inquiry of a lady on a ladder painting the ceiling, I said, "This is she." He was a devoted supporter from that moment.

The "It takes a village" concept continued in California. As previously explained, in order to implement the PAL Center, Belva Holder and other community individuals were key components. After securing a building, and applying for funds to operate a program, it was necessary to seek computers and operating equipment. Having learned that the way to obtain funds was to apply for a grant, I submitted a proposal to the San Bernardino County Community Services Department (CSD), under the direction of Ms. Patricia Nichols. Through funding from the CSD, we were able to purchase our first two computers. We applied the following year and secured two more computers from CSD. We met with the Kiwanis Club of San Bernardino, and with the assistance of Mr. Alfred Jenkins, we were funded to purchase two more units.

Through funding sources and donations, we were able to secure new and used equipment for our computer lab. We requested the help of Danny Tillman to repair our computers. He relates how he came to "this old, dilapidated building" and seeing our outdated equipment, he assisted in securing resources. Mr. Tillman was later elected to the San Bernardino City Unified School District Board of Education. We also called on Walter (Walt) Hawkins at California State University who helped with our electronic needs, did the research for our proposals, and helped write the Talent Search Grant.

George Lee became Chief Operating Officer and brought in excellent staff additions such as our current CEO, Dwaine Radden, Sr., who is determined to carry on the legacy of PAL Center's dedication and community services. We began as a tutoring program and expanded to over 20 different community-based programs and services. We also added a second PAL Charter Academy campus in San Bernardino.

The Hood to the Hill

The PAL Center affiliates wanted to help students from low-income areas realize they could finish high school and go to college. When I wanted to secure a U.S. Department of Education Talent Search Program for the PAL Center, I went to Mr. Walter Hawkins and his wife, Professor Jean Peacock, who was Director of The Student Assistance in Learning (SAIL) Program at CSUSB. Walter and Jean were instrumental in the PAL Center obtaining the grant. We worked weekends and Jean actually hand-wrote the proposal, on legal pads! This amazed me since my handwriting was atrocious and I probably would have developed hand cramps.

We worked weekends and the community owes Jean, Walter, and Dr. Tom Rivera, CSUSB Department Head, many thanks and gratitude for their time and use of facilities to seek and provide this successful program in the community. Dr. Rivera, who is wheelchair-bound, was very supportive of activities that would help the youth in the community. Through the Talent Search Grant, we provided tutoring and educational college-bound services to 1,000 students each year for six years in various schools in the San Bernardino and Rialto School Districts. This was the precursor to our U.S. Department of Education Upward Bound Programs, which provided college-bound educational assistance to students in the San Bernardino, Rialto, and Fontana Unified School Districts.

Students could see the pipeline from middle school to college through the TRIO programs. During the summer months, seniors who were enrolled in our college preparation, Upward Bound Program stayed in the dormitories and attended classes at CSUSB and on other college campuses. The goal was to be immersed in the college experience. Few nonprofit organizations across the country operated programs of this magnitude in their communities.

Talent Search provided college-bound activities for middle school students. Upward Bound is designed for high school students who wish to go to college, and the third arm of the TRIO Program is a college campus organization to guide and support students through their college years to graduation. At CSUSB, this program is the SAIL (Student Assistance in Learning) Program. The PAL Center was successful in obtaining grants for two Upward Bound programs which we operated for years. Before that, we operated the Talent Search Program for six years. These programs are usually located on university and college campuses.

The PAL Center, since its inception, has been a pioneer in providing educational programs and assistance to area youth, whether at the community level or in the local unified school districts.

XXIV

COMMUNITY-BASED PROGRAMS

We wrote grants and secured funding to provide services for various community needs. For dropout prevention and recovery, we started Operation RETAIN (Rescue Educational Training and Initiative Now). We established community-based services which were accessible to those most in need. In order to fight pregnancies, we implemented "TEENS FOR RESPONSIBLE BEHAVIOR." To fight drugs and gangs we supported the play, "CRACKDOWN," brought to us by Reuben Herndon, which was shown free of charge to requesting schools. We published a comic book, MIGHTY MEDIC VS THE DOPE DEMON, A "SMART MEDIC RAP" written by PAL Center employee, Clarence Vernardo, and funded by the U.S. Department of Education. We also wrote a grant and operated a traveling mobile, SUBSTANCE ABUSE MOBILE (SAM II), patterned after a Washington, D.C. program. An RV that traveled to street corners, churches, and schools, we displayed the detrimental effect of drugs and gang involvement. Pasadena Community College requested an additional day on campus when we took our mobile unit there.

For homeless youth returning to old environments, we wrote a proposal for a transitional living project, OPERATION SAFE HARBOR, which provided independent living skills training to youth 18 years of age who were aging out of the system. At the PAL Center we saw problems and instead of an "evolution of excuses," we implemented an "evolution of performance." Our original OPERATION RETAIN educational tutoring program eventually evolved into the PAL Charter Academy, the first charter school approved by the San Bernardino City Unified School District. In addition to the charter high school, we operated a Child Care Center, tutoring programs for the probation department and school district, after-school programs, and Talent Search and Upward Bound college-going programs. The PAL Center had 11 different programs operating simultaneously.

The successes were many. Residents of our homeless Operation Safe Harbor program graduated high school, and some residents went to community college. The Upward Bound Program sent 100% of its students to college, with 27 seniors graduating in 2002, 19 in 2003, 17 in 2004. Homeless students were reunited with their families. Through our youth employment program, we placed probation youth in environments such as the library at the CSUSB University where one of our participants, a male ex-gang member, was proclaimed the best worker ever received. CSUSB was a worksite for numerous students. In 1990 we had 10 students placed there, including 15-year-old Amy Harper, whose supervisor, Mrs. Lois Hill stated in the <u>CALIFORNIA STATE UNIVERSITY SAN BERNARDINO THE FRIDAY BULLETIN, JULY 1990</u>: "It has been a joy working with Amy Harper. She was eager to learn the various duties in that department from the acquisition of the journals to shelving them. I'm sure she will do well in her future endeavors." Amy also derived benefits from the program. "I earn money and I really want to go to college."

The Kiwanis Club sponsored a key club at our charter school, supported homeless youth for an annual award, and sponsored PAL students at California Boys State. We had PAL program graduates gainfully employed in such places as the San Bernardino City Mayor's Office.

Programs were successful from the beginning. For instance, PROJECT EARLY OUTREACH enrolled 131 students from January 1 to June 30, 1986. Students came from 19 San Bernardino City United School District elementary schools.

Other interesting statistics are observed in our OPERATION RETAIN academic program. In 1990, of 100 enrollees, 64% were male. In our TEENS FOR RESPONSIBLE BEHAVIOR program, 79% were male. Of the 88 students enrolled in the ALTERNATIVE STREET ACADEMY program, funded by the San Bernardino City Unified School District, 84% were male. Of the 90 youths enrolled in the PAL Center's JTPA PROJECT EARN AND LEARN Summer Youth Employment Program, 84% of enrollees were male. In 1993-94, of 56 students enrolled in the TRAINING, INTERNSHIP, AND PLACEMENT PROGRAM, 52% were male. All 100% were placed on jobs. In 1992 we enrolled 1,002 students in our TALENT SEARCH program, and in 1993 we enrolled 1,005 middle school students in the PAL Center's Talent Search college preparatory program. We provided academic enrichment and college preparatory services to over 1,000 students in the San Bernardino, Rialto, and Fontana school districts each year for six years, prior to being awarded our UPWARD BOUND grants.

The diversity of our programs also made us unique. Each year our graduates and commencement speakers have been outstanding. In 2012, the PAL Charter Academy graduated 82 students with High School Diplomas (HSD), and 9 students earned General Education Diplomas (GED).

Project Early Outreach

We held free tutoring sessions on Saturday mornings at the PAL Center and in the Public Enterprise Building on Highland Avenue. This nice brick building was mostly vacant and owned by The City of San Bernardino. Before I arrived in San Bernardino, I understand that this beautiful building, secured through the efforts of Mrs. Francis Grice and others, had been a vocational training building.

Students from California State University provided PAL Center tutoring to the community's children as part of their fieldwork experience. It was a very successful program with parents thankful and grateful for the help provided for the elementary school children. Coordinator, Sharon Atkins took elementary students who had never been out of their neighborhoods on field trips to Cal State University, a Creamery, Knotts Berry Farm, Puppet Shows at the Public Library, and other enlightening ventures. Our programs were so effective we needed to expand.

The Public Enterprise building was primarily empty, and the PAL Center was in need of additional space. I remembered the Biblical walk around the Jericho walls. The Jericho participants marched around the walls seven times, blew the loud horn, and the walls collapsed. The Biblical adage was to walk around something that one wanted seven times and then claim it. I wanted that building so badly that I walked around the building seven times and claimed it. However, we did not get possession of the building. That claim was not honored. Perhaps I needed to blow the loud horn.

Following the unsuccessful "claim it" experience, the New Hope Baptist Church loaned us one of their houses on Medical Center Drive in order to expand our program. One year later we relocated to State Street and Highland Avenue so that all operations could be housed under one roof.

We have operated more than 11 programs simultaneously in various categories that provided High School Diplomas, GED's, English as a Second Language, Adult Basic Education (ABE), Youth Vocational Training and Employment, Safe Harbor Youth Homeless Shelters, Talent Search, and Upward Bound college preparatory programs, Child Care and Development Center, Creative Before and After School programs for Success (CAPS), GAIN, Temporary Assistance for Needy Families (TANF), and CalWORKs welfare reform programs, "Teens for Responsible Behavior," (SAM) Substance Abuse Mobile

(SAM II) gang intervention program, and numerous other programs that drew national recognition. We supported the anti-gang, anti-drug play "CRACKDOWN," and was federally funded to perform free of charge to requesting schools. SAM II, the anti-gang mobile/anti-drug mobile traveling unit was so popular that Pasadena Community College requested we stay overnight for an additional showing on their campus. SAM II was also shown on TV. The Upward Bound students visited the Museum of Tolerance in Los Angeles, in addition to numerous college campuses. The community and conservation were involved in the PAL Center's Lytle Creek Watershed Action Project, to preserve and restore conservation, and in the Southern California Edison VOICE community service project. In addition to academic programs, we offered vocational programs such as culinary arts and construction. We planted gardens and taught the students how to grow food and survive.

We have had as many as 50 employees on staff at one time, many of whom returned to school and furthered their education. One Project Early Outreach motivated teacher, finished college, went to law school, and became an attorney with the US Department of Labor. Excellent teachers and staff members have provided unparalleled service to the community for over 35 years. Two former public-school principals came out of retirement when we were in need. Mr. Huey Dredd, also a product of Arkansas, heeded our call, and Mrs. Lynette Forte came out of retirement twice.

Many PAL staff members and graduates entered the teaching profession or other gainful employment. The old axiom "drop a pebble in the water" and see how far the ripples reverberate is most applicable to the PAL Center's involvement in the community. Longevity was also a staple among many employees. Business Manager, Tammie Hicks Amis-Jackson, employed for 32 loyal years and still going strong, was hired as a secretary at age 19. Lawrence Hampton joined the staff in 1988 and retired in 2015 after 27 years of dedicated service.

Understanding adversity was a guiding force in providing services to lesser advantaged populations.

XXV

PERSON TO PROFESSION

As I reflect on activities at the PAL Center, I recall events and activities that led me to this point. These events made me very sensitive to children learning and performing.

My children were quite active in school and events. Noteworthy, was a piano duet and singing by my children, Alvia and Angelo, at Maxwell Elementary school. Later, Angelo was the first chair trumpet player at St. Paul Park High School. Citing a Clinic of the Minnesota Music Educators Association, held in St. Paul's new Hilton Hotel, the daily newspaper stated that "A HIGHLIGHT OF THE PROGRAM IS A BRILLIANT TRUMPET SOLO, SPECIALLY ARRANGED WITH BAND ACCOMPANIMENT BY MR. BUDAHL AND PLAYED BY ANGELO HAMPTON, THE BAND'S 1ST TRUMPSTER." The band was composed of selected musicians from two junior high schools. The suicide of this talented youngster made me wonder how I could help youth with their problems. Hence, the PAL Center. Hopefully, no other youngster will feel hopeless.

Life Changer

The suicide death of our oldest child, Angelo Jerome, at age 15, was a life-changer. Suicide was an unbelievable occurrence in my cultural environment. I knew absolutely nothing about suicidal tendencies. Angelo seemed to be a musical and happy child. However, there were emotional problems with which he apparently felt unable to cope. It is because of Angelo that I changed my life profession from my college major of music to counseling when I went to graduate school. It was too late to save my child, but I determined to save others. I became a professional counselor educator in order to help others counsel youth. Many youths who go to the PAL Center are in need of role models and counseling.

Angelo's death also had a profound effect on the children. I later learned that they were teased at school because of the tragedy. We were the only African American family in the area and the article was in the newspaper. At that time, Angelo was enrolled at St. Thomas Military Academy, was the lead trumpeter, and was usually sent to play taps for funerals.

With such a tragic environment and no apparent reconciliation of parental thinking, I decided to temporarily move the children to a happier, family-supported environment in Arkansas. I opted to enroll them in school in Pine Bluff. My youngest son, Lawrence, has vivid memories of his travels from Minnesota to Arkansas to California. He relives the pleasant and unpleasant memories of Minnesota and my experiences as an abused homemaker to the family breadwinner. He recalls the move from a single-family four-bedroom walkout rambler in Minnesota to a farmhouse which was temporarily shared by four families. It was a crowded but pleasant, memorable experience.

The children continued their school activities in Pine Bluff. Alvia played tenor saxophone in marching, jazz, and concert bands, and flute in the symphonic band. Lawrence played baritone horn at Southeast Junior High and ran track at Pine Bluff High. Pam played tenor saxophone, ran track, and was a 7th grade cheerleader. She was also a majorette for Carver Elementary School. Delano played bass clarinet in the band before returning to Minnesota. All siblings entered college and received a Bachelor of Science degree. Alvia finished at the University of Arkansas at Pine Bluff; Lawrence finished Southern Illinois University at Edwardsville; Pam finished Texas Woman's University (TWU) in Denton Texas, and Delano finished the University of Minnesota in Minneapolis. All received recognitions such as Lawrence was included in WHO'S WHO AMONG STUDENTS IN AMERICAN COLLEGES AND UNIVERSITIES, and OUTSTANDING YOUNG MEN OF AMERICA. Alvia was in WHO'S WHO AMONG STUDENTS IN AMERICAN COLLEGES AND UNIVERSITIES and WHO'S WHO AMONG AMERICAN TEACHERS. Pam was selected "Ms. Essence" at TWU, sang in the Ensemble, and was published in the NATIONAL DEAN'S HONOR ROLL for years.

A magazine article was published about Del, "AFFIRMATIVE IN ACTION," in the Minneapolis-St. Paul Magazine, when he was a sales representative for a food service restaurant supplier. He was also a noted part-time waiter at Brown and Bigelow at the Sheraton Midway.

My son, Lawrence, and I both finished Southern Illinois University Edwardsville, and in 1983 Lawrence drove me from Arkansas to California to my new job at California State University San Bernardino. He returned to Arkansas and later came back to California as Administrator at the PAL Center in San Bernardino from 1988 to 2015 when he established his own private tennis business, GAME SET MATCH. Lawrence brought his skills from Minnesota to Arkansas to California to the PAL Center.

XXVI

SIGNIFICANT EVENTS

There were many significant events along the journey.

1988

In a letter dated March 28, 1988, from the Congress of the United States Joint Economic Committee, I was invited to Washington by Congressman Augustus F. Hawkins, Chairman of Subcommittee on Investment, Jobs, and Prices, to testify at The Committee Hearing in Washington, D.C. on April 18, 1988. I was asked to testify in the Rayburn House Office Building on (1) the strengths and shortcomings of existing national policy in education, employment, and training; (2) the problems of dropout-youth and their efforts to become financially independent based on criminal activity; and (3) the kinds of partnerships and innovations necessary to meet the challenges of a changing labor market through the year 2000. Twenty copies of written testimony were submitted and distributed to Committee Members and staff, and "printed in full in the hearing record." An additional 50 copies were requested for distribution to the press and other interested parties.

1995

In 1995, the year of my retirement, I was the Grand Marshal for California State University at San Bernardino's commencement. I carried The Holy Grail and led the professors and faculty into the commencement arena. I also sat on the platform with the CSUSB president and other privileged guests.

I was asked to serve as a reader of proposals for three Federal Agencies. As a reader for Federal proposals, it meant going to Washington rather frequently. Each time that I went, I visited politicians "on the hill." Proposal readers were usually brought in on Sunday and we read proposals Sunday through Thursday. Many readers left on Thursday afternoon and Friday morning, however, I usually stayed over on Friday to make political contacts, to let politicians know that we were in town, and to seek opportunities for PAL Center recognition and growth.

1996

In 1996, I went to Washington, D.C. twice as a proposal reader, in July and again in September. I met with Congressman Frank Riggs, in the Longworth Building, and with California 40th District Congressman Jerry Lewis, and with California 47th District Congressman George Brown in the Rayburn Building. I also met with officials of Congressman Major Owens of New York; and California Senators Dianne Feinstein and Barbara Boxer in the Hart Building. I made the rounds.

It was through these contacts that I was invited to Washington by U. S. Representative Charles Hayes, First Congressional District, Illinois to be a Workshop Panelist on DROPOUTS-PUSHOUTS-TECHNOLOGIES FOR THE '90S. The workshop was at the 17th Annual Legislative Weekend of the Congressional Black Caucus Foundation. My topic was "COMMUNITY-BASED ORGANIZATIONS AND THEIR EFFORTS TO ADDRESS THE DROPOUT PROBLEM."

1997-98

I went to Washington D.C. in 1997, and again in August 1998. Each time that I went, I met with legislators. In 1998, in addition to California Congressmen Brown and Lewis, I met with New York Congressman Charles Rangel and was invited to his televised session on drug abuse. A former Arkansan, I visited the office of Senator Dale Bumpers and found out that a secretary in his office was the daughter of my former classmate, Ruby Jewel Lyons Holland at Merrill High School in Pine Bluff, Arkansas.

The Washington housing experiences were varied. In 1996, I stayed at the St. James Residence in Georgetown, which had an English motif. I liked the atmosphere and stayed there whenever I had a choice. However, most times, especially when reading proposals, the government made all arrangements at a specific hotel.

Vacations

In 1998, I managed to get in some vacation time. Sister Vhaness and I left for Orlando, Florida on Sunday, September 20, 1998. Our destination was The Bahamas; however, we flew into Orlando and rented a car to drive to Fort Lauderdale to board the ship. We wanted to see the Cape Canaveral/Kennedy Space LaunchPad. We drove to Fort Lauderdale at a time when hurricane George was headed for Florida. We decided to skip the cruise; briefly visited Miami, Florida; returned to the hotel in Fort Lauderdale; drove through Disney World at Orlando; and then to the Orlando Airport to board the airplane for Ontario and the safety of California. I was so tired of the drive and tour, that I fell asleep in the airport lying on one of the tables. Vhaness was awake, however, and took a photo of me asleep on the table. We did not miss the flight, even though we lost the money paid for the cruise, our lives were intact.

We returned to California on Thursday, and on the following Sunday, we left for Washington, D.C. to attend the CEO America Inc (CEOA) Conference. It was at this conference that I met Mr. William "Bill" Clarke, who became the proposal writer for our successful Upward Bound programs.

Proposal Frenzy

In 1998, we submitted numerous proposals which required working late into the night many, many times. Lawrence, Tammie, and I worked in the PAL Center conference room at 10 and 11 PM, then rushed to the post office in Redlands, California at 11:30 P.M. in order to have the proposal stamped by the midnight deadline. These proposals included CDBG proposals, Talent Search proposals, Job Training, and Partnership Act (JTPA) proposals, Upward Bound, Summer Youth Employment Training, Greater Avenues to Independence (GAIN), CalWorks, the Transitional Living and the Safe Harbor programs, and others.

2000

CHARTER SCHOOL PETITION

The PAL Center's academic department had previously worked with the Colton, Fontana, and Snowline Unified School Districts providing high school diplomas and educational services. When the Snowline School District in Phelan, California reformatted its structure to implement a charter school, we decided to submit a proposal to the San Bernardino City Unified School District to operate our own charter school. Lawrence Hampton, the PAL Center's Administrator, and I met with Snowline Superintendent, Dr. Eric Johnson, in February 2000, and announced our intent to sever the relationship and apply with our local school district to pursue our educational collaborations. I researched the charter movement, studied several charter proposals, and wrote a proposal for Provisional Educational Services, Incorporated to petition the San Bernardino City Unified School District to operate a charter school. In preparing the charter proposal for the San Bernardino City Unified School District, our primary contact was Dr. Narcisco Cardonna. Dr. Cardonna was a guiding force through the process. The charter proposal was submitted to the San Bernardino City Unified School District on April 3, 2000 and approved on July 18, 2000. On May 5, 2000, we also submitted the proposal to the U.S. Department of Health and Human Services for the first successful Safe Harbor Program for homeless youth.

The Hurricane

The month of June was a milestone in the San Bernardino area. Coordinated by our Public Relations employee, Lea Cash, our PAL Center graduation speaker in June 2000 was Ruben "The Hurricane" Carter of the movie "THE HURRICANE," starring Denzel Washington. Mr. Carter arrived on Thursday evening and graduation was held on Friday. The Precinct Reporter Newspaper sponsored a reception for Mr. Carter on Friday evening and also sponsored a book signing on Saturday morning. Mr. Carter left immediately for Canada after the ceremonies. Some authorities in the United States are still seeking to re-arrest him for the crime of murder for which he was exonerated and proven to be wrongly convicted as a child.

The Canadian Excursion

On July 1st, Vhaness and I went to Toronto, Canada to visit Ruben "The Hurricane" Carter and his "wrongly convicted" program. We returned to California on July 10. While in Canada we stayed at the Broadgate Arms, a residence and hotel combination. It was a very informative visit. We visited the Casa Loma Castle, had dinner in the beautiful flower gardens at Reuben's home, visited the United States side of Niagara Falls, and had dinner in the CNN Tower revolving restaurant. We rode the ferry along the Queens Quay, and then it was back to California and reality.

Charter Petition Approved

On July 18, 2000, at the San Bernardino City Unified School District Board of Education meeting, our charter proposal was accepted, and Provisional Educational Services Inc. was approved to begin and operate the first charter school under the auspices of the San Bernardino City Unified School District.

Congressman Mervyn (Merv) Dynmally, a longtime legislative representative of California's 31st Congressional District, heard of our successful venture to operate a charter school and visited our campus in San Bernardino. He invited us to come to Compton Community College in Los Angeles to assess the possibilities of beginning a program there. We met with the president, however, at that time Compton college was just exploring and our program was too new to be implemented elsewhere. Congressman Dynmally subsequently brought a lady who wanted to begin a charter school to visit our PAL facility.

The Congressman also donated a piece of San Bernardino property to Provisional Educational Services, Incorporated on State Street. Dr. Dynmally was supportive of the PAL Center through the efforts of George Lee, a PAL Center employee, who was a student of Congressman Dynmally while attending Roger Mudd College in Claremont, California.

Additional traveling and contacts occurred when I attended the National Charter School Conference at the Omni Shores Hotel in Washington D.C. in December 2000. While there I met with Dr. Jane Smith President of the National Council of Negro Women, and Congressman Joe Baca of the 43rd Congressional District.

2001
Lupus Claims Pamela Jeanne
The year 2001 began with the heart-wrenching death of my youngest child Pamela Jeanne Hampton-Ross. Pam had been fighting the dreaded disease of lupus for years and finally lost the battle. She earned her Master's degree, was employed, became an entrepreneur as her health deteriorated, and finally succumbed. Pam was taken to the hospital by ambulance Thursday, January 25 at approximately 6:30 PM. Lawrence and I were notified by daughter Alvia, and I left for Dallas on a midnight flight. Arriving at approximately 10:30 A.M. Friday, when the taxi

driver finally found the facility, Pam was unconscious, on a ventilator, and not expected to survive.

Pam was tested on Sunday for brain activity and again on Monday morning. There was no activity and, reportedly, according to an agreement between Pam and husband Charles, he consented for her to be removed from life support. Pam was declared dead at 3:05 P.M. at Arlington Medical Center. The funeral of my youngest child was held at Faith Baptist Church in Grand Prairie, Texas on Saturday, February 3 with interment at Moore Cemetery in Arlington, Texas. February 4TH was my birthday.

Pam will not be alone in Texas. Son Delano suggested, and we concurred and purchased a family site of seven plots. It is a beautiful well-kept site with waterspouts and a small lake. This will assure family togetherness and a place of rest for each family member desiring to be placed there. I have selected this site for my final journey.

TRAVEL TO EUROPE

In order to relieve some of the stress, my son Del took me on a vacation to Europe - to London, England, and Paris, France. I joined Del in Minneapolis, Minnesota, and toured some of the old sites where we formerly lived, such as downtown St. Paul and Woodbury. I also saw the beautiful fruit and flower gardens that Del had planted in Minneapolis. He had gardens at two of his houses, and community gardens in downtown Minneapolis.

It was most interesting to see Delano's gardens because as children, my little ones worked in gardens, whether on the farm in Arkansas, in the garden in St. Paul, Minnesota, in Woodbury, Minnesota, and wherever we lived. They vowed that they would never work in a garden when they "grew up." However, each child in adulthood, has a garden. In Minnesota, Del, in fact, entered his award-winning flowers in the Minnesota State Fair, and elsewhere, and won many awards. Upon retirement, Del also became a master gardener, employed by the University of Minnesota.

Leaving for Europe, we took the 8-hour flight to London, England. Upon arrival, we signed up for the double-decker "Big Bus Tour" of London. While in London, we visited the Tower of London, the Museum, The Square, St. Paul Cathedral, The University of London, Piccadilly Circle, and rode the Millennial Wheel. We went to Buckingham Palace, saw "The Changing of the Guards," took a boat ride on the Thames River to Westminster, visited Harrod's Department where Princess Diane is memorialized, and saw 24 other tourist attractions and stops. We were in London, England May 17th and 18th. and left for Paris, France on May 19th riding the Eurostar train under the English Channel.

After checking into the Holiday Inn, Del said he had a "surprise." We took a train to the famous *EIFFEL TOWER*, where Del and I went to the top! We bought a 2-day pass on the "L'OpenTour Bus" – a double-decker with an open upper deck, where we sat. We visited such places as the fabulous Sacré-Coeur Basilica, Cathédrale Notre-Dame and the Sainte-Chapelle, The Sorbonne and the University of Paris, the Musee du Louvre, Moulin Rouge, Luxembourg Palace, took a boat ride on the famous Seine River, and visited other tourist attractions. We visited sites in Paris Monday, Tuesday, and Wednesday, returning to London, under the English Channel, on the Eurostar train on Thursday, May 24th. We departed London, England, and arrived in Minneapolis, Minneapolis on Friday, May 25th. What a trip!

2002

The main fundraiser for the PAL Center was the annual golf tournament which began in May 2002. In addition to the golf tournament, other activities were used to supplement our program. For instance, when the Mervyns Department Store clothes closet came to San Bernardino, our students who were enrolled in the GAIN welfare reform program were treated to a visit to the Mervyn mobile unit in April 2003, where they were fitted with new outfits at no cost.

Another fundraising event was coordinated by George Lee when Judge Maybelline of the TV program of the same name was brought to San Bernardino as a fundraiser for the PAL Center. Golf Tournaments, however, were our biggest fundraisers. Accepting the idea of chief instigator Artis Gilbert, we held annual golf tournaments for eight consecutive years.

Staff retreats at resort areas for nonprofit organizations were very rare at that time. We were fortunate enough to have a Corporate Board President, Rick Stiles, who invited us to come on August 2002 to his resort home at Laughlin, Nevada, on the Mississippi River. It was quite an enjoyable experience.

2003

During the month of February, there were always numerous speaking engagements. One notable appearance was for The Navy Chiefs, in Victorville California, arranged by Retired Chief Petty Officer Harold Gilbert.

Mrs. Margaret Hill, Principal of San Andreas High School and a staunch supporter of the PAL Center, retired from the school district. Subsequently, Mrs. Hill won a seat on the San Bernardino City Unified School District Board of Education and was awarded an honorary doctorate degree from the University of Redlands. Dr. Hill mentored the first principal at the PAL Charter Academy High School, Tom Cass.

During the year 2003, we operated two Safe Harbor programs for homeless youth. One shelter was located in Rialto and the other in San Bernardino. The original Safe Harbor program was funded and implemented on Foothill Boulevard in the City of Fontana at an empty motel site.

After being awarded the grants for the Upward Bound and Talent Search programs, I became a reader for three U. S. Department Governmental Agencies: The U. S Department of Education, The Department of Health and Human Services, and The U.S. Department of Youth and

Family Services. At one of the evaluations, while reading proposals for the U.S. Department of Youth and Family Services, I was enthralled with the idea of providing shelters for 18-year-old and older homeless youth who were aging out of the foster care and/or probation systems.

I brought the idea of a homeless shelter for youth to the PAL Center, we researched, wrote a proposal, submitted it, and were funded to operate <u>OPERATION SAFE HARBOR</u>, a shelter for homeless youth. A benefit of being a governmental reader is that you get ideas. One cannot take proposals from the site, however, ideas can be taken back, shared, and successfully written proposals may be funded. Subsequent to the funding, we found an empty former motel on Foothill Boulevard in the City of Fontana where we implemented Operation Safe Harbor. The facility had an office and kitchen facilities in front and double occupancy bedrooms for each participant. We had an on-site director, Dr. Carl Moore, a chiropractor, who lived in a modular unit on the Fontana site. It was through Dr. Moore and his contact that we brought to San Bernardino the reigning 1990 Ms. Black Teenage World, Debelah Morgan.

Mrs. Georgia Morris, a longtime member and secretary of Provisional Educational Services, Inc., was very enthusiastic about this program and provided much of the bedding, curtains, and kitchen utensils to prepare the living quarters for the residents. Monitoring young adult males, and security, at that facility, however, proved to be quite a challenge. Consequently, after about one year, we secured a two-story house and moved the program to the City of Rialto. Because of the great need, we wrote another proposal and received the funding to provide an additional homeless shelter for youth. The Safe Harbor II program was implemented in the City of San Bernardino.

2004
In 2004, some charter schools that were affiliated with the Victorville Snowline Unified School District were experiencing legal difficulties and the directors asked to affiliate with the PAL Center. The Director of The Public Safety Academy, Michael Dickinson, which had been affiliated with a Snowline program in Victorville, came to a PESI Board meeting, with parents, and asked to affiliate with the PAL Center. We agreed and they retained their program at the Norton Air Force Base site in San Bernardino, with oversight from the PAL Center in Muscoy.

In August, we were approached by Zachary Fox of Inland Christian Center Church of Colton to affiliate their charter school with the PAL Center and Charter Academy. We agreed to provide oversight.

Manny Aranda, an active member of the Redlands Kiwanis Club, and President of the PAL Academy Board of Trustees was instrumental in starting a Key Club for the students on the PAL Charter Academy campus.
The principal of the PAL Charter Academy at that time was Tom Cass, my former student at CSUSB. As the first

charter school in San Bernardino, we were trailblazers and set numerous precedents.

The year 2004 was also a notable year for African American females in education. The Superintendent of the Rialto School District was Ms. Edna Herring, a former Principal of Rialto's Eisenhower High School. The district also named a new school the Wilmer Carter High School, after Assembly Member Wilmer "Amina" Carter, California 62nd Assembly District.

2005
The Motherland
In December 2005, I had the privilege of traveling to "The Motherland" of Ghana, West Africa. I always knew that I was a descendent of kings and queens, not the savages portrayed in American movies. I had long wanted to visit Africa and instead of waiting for a group tour, I contacted a former classmate of AM&N college, Kofi Addo, who lived in Ghana. Mr. Addo had traveled from Ghana to America on a steamboat to get an education in America and ended up at AM&N College where he was an outstanding student. Kofi had returned to Ghana and worked with the Ghanaian Government in Africa and London, England.

This exciting contact with Kofi Addo resulted in a tour company contacting me and making all arrangements for the visit. I left Ontario, California airport on Thursday, December 8th, traveling to Minneapolis where I joined a fellow traveler to go to Accra, Ghana. The traveler was

Gloria Mensah, the niece of Mr. Addo who was raised as his daughter and lived in England at the time. She was traveling to Ghana for the Christmas holidays. Luckily, Gloria was with me, because she knew the culture and negotiated our entry into the country. I would have been absolutely lost without her.

My son, Del, picked us up at the Minneapolis - St. Paul Airport and we went to Mid-America Mall, the largest mall in the country. We returned to the airport and left for Amsterdam on KLM Dutch Airlines arriving in Amsterdam at noon the next day. We left Amsterdam on Friday, December 9th, at 2:20 P.M. arriving in Accra, Ghana at 8:45 P.M. where we were met by Gloria's family and the word "Akwaaba" (Welcome) prominently displayed in the absolutely spotless airport!

The trip was fantastic, and Kofi arranged everything. I arrived in the **ACCRA REGION**. Saturday, I was taken by taxi to the University of Ghana to attend a 50th Anniversary Celebration of the primary school on the campus and the dedication of the library to Gloria's deceased mother. Kofi had arranged for my own private tour guide, Volkswagen minivan, and driver for all seven days of the tour.

On Sunday we drove on the only concrete road built by President Nkrumah, past numerous villages, and went to Akosombo to the **VOLTA REGION,** to see Lake Volta, the largest man-made lake in the world. I cruised the lake on "The Princess" which had a live band, dancing, and lunch, and visited the "Captains Bridge," where I actually piloted the boat. We saw native dancers on Dido Island and returned to Akosombo to spend the night at the Continental Hotel, where my second-floor balcony room had a beautiful view of Volta Lake. On Monday, we journeyed to Wli Waterfalls, the highest waterfalls in Ghana. The falls is known locally as Agoomatsa Waterfalls - meaning, "Allow Me to Flow." We trekked one hour through the jungle, across 10 bridges, to the base of the waterfall. I saw many things such as coffee plants, cassava, mongo, cocoa, cashew, red oil palm, and silk-cotton trees. We continued to the highest mountain in Ghana, Mount Afadja.

Tuesday was a city tour where I saw Nkrumah Memorial Park and Mausoleum, where the first president of Ghana, President Kwame Nkrumah stood to declare independence. I also shopped at the African markets. We paid a courtesy call to the American Embassy where I visited with U.S. Ambassador, Her Excellency, Pamela Bridgeport.

Wednesday, we departed for Kumasi and the **ASHANTI REGION.** We had a rest-stop and lunch near the mountain where Nana Kofi Addo is a Tribal Chief. His people are the Kwahu tribe. My tour guide, Yaw, went to a boarding high school for five years on that mountaintop. We toured Central Market, one of the largest in West Africa. I had dinner with Mr. Addo, who had flown from Accra to introduce me to the King the next day, however the King's

Sister died, and he was in mourning. The dinner and overnight stay was at the Pink Panther Hotel.

On Thursday, we toured the Manhyia Palace and visited the Okomfo Anokye Sword Site, where a sword is said to have been plunged into the ground by a priest in the year 1695. To this day no one has been able to pull it out of the ground. I tried.

On Friday, we visited Elmina in the **CENTRAL REGION** and visited Kakum National Park which has one of the four swinging bridges in the world. One can cross seven bridges above the treetops of the rain forest to get to the other side. The four canopies are found in Malaysia, China, Peru, and Ghana. Ghana has the highest and longest at 355 meters long and 40 meters high. I hasten to say that I looked but did not cross. We drove through the large gold mining town of Obuasi to the Cape Coast Castle, the seat of British Government since 1652, until Independence in 1957. The castle occupies approximately 73,600 sq. ft. I walked through dungeons, tunnels, prison cells, and saw cannons and cannonballs on the castle walls. Cape Coast is the capital of the Central Region.

I stayed overnight at the Elmina Beach Resort Hotel where my second-story room and balcony were right on the Atlantic Ocean. The town of Elmina dates back to the 1300s.

On Saturday, I had a guided tour of the Elmina Castle which was built by the Portuguese in 1482. Christopher

Columbus spent the night in the castle before coming to America. I saw the female and male dungeons, cells, trapdoors where female slaves were brought up for the pleasure of the governor, and most memorable was "THE DOOR OF NO RETURN." This is where slaves were taken down to the boats to be shipped to America.

A group of students were learning history at Elmina Castle. All primary and secondary students wear uniforms, including shirts and ties. While traveling, I noticed a goat traveling on top of a public transportation bus. Another memorable scene was a 12-year-old girl carrying on her head a huge basket of bread for sale.

We returned to Accra where the dressmaker came with five outfits that she made for me in one week. My tour guide, Yaw, shared additional tidbits such as one's first name represents the day on which you were born, i.e., Kofi is born on Wednesday, and Kwame is born on Friday. Brothers and sisters of your parents are not your aunt and uncles. Ladies are all mothers and men are all fathers, e.g., when you walk into a family home, a child may address all three men as "daddy." In the culture, I am addressed as "Mother Mildred."

On Sunday, Chief Addo picked me up in a taxi and we attended Ridge Church with Kofi's daughter Kay and family. Chief Addo also took me to the Holy Trinity Cathedral where the Archbishop was conducting service. We observed an ordination service, received communion from the Archbishop, and I was asked to speak briefly (surprise, surprise) to the congregation.

Monday, the tour guide and driver picked me up for an additional tour of Accra, and for which they refused to charge. We visited the Dr. W. E. B. DuBois Museum, the tombs of George Padmore, an activist, and Dr. Kwame Nkrumah, all leaders in the Pan-African movement. I saw Dr. DuBois' Harvard doctoral robe, his artifacts, and sat at one of Dr. DuBois' tables. We observed the culture of Ghana, Independence Square, Government Buildings, and the National Theater, a very modern, beautiful architectural design building.

On Tuesday, I packed, and Kofi arrived with a taxi. I had lunch with Kofi's daughter, Kay who took me to the airport where I met Kofi's daughter, Gloria, in the immigration line. We boarded a huge plane for Amsterdam at 11:05 PM. From Amsterdam, Gloria left for Minneapolis, and one and a half hours later, I left for Los Angeles, arriving at 1:45 PM. The flight from Amsterdam to Los Angeles was 11 hours in the air.

In Africa, it was a very sobering experience to stand in "THE DOOR OF NO RETURN" and visualize my people being herded to the boats below in the shadow of the huge cannons that were perched on the castle walls. We were told that rebellious slaves were placed in the cells in which I stood and left to die. Sometimes bodies were not removed until all had died. Just to imagine this inhuman treatment is mind-boggling. For my people to survive these intolerable inflictions is a testimony to the unyielding human spirit.

WHAT A MEMORABLE TRIP TO "THE MOTHERLAND!"

I returned from Ghana on December 20 and left for Texas for the Christmas and New Year holidays on December 24.

2006
Family members have always been active in sports. For instance, both granddaughters, Mizz and Misti Turner ran track. Misti ran in the Texas Relays, and in April 2006 I attended that event. Misti later attended George Mason University in Virginia on a track scholarship. Lawrence ran track at Pine Bluff High School and received an athletic letter in that sport.

A highlight of the year 2006 was "FOOTSTEPS TO FREEDOM," a tour on the Underground Railroad (UGRR) which began Sunday, July 9. On this trip, we traveled the path of slaves who escaped to freedom. The tour was sponsored by the Black Voice Foundation in San Bernardino, and Kenley Konnection, a full-service travel agency in Ohio.

Led by Cheryl Brown, owner of THE VOICE NEWSPAPER, we boarded the airplane in Ontario, California on Sunday, July 9th, for Columbus, Ohio where we were met with a beautiful 2006 motorcoach, in which we traveled to Maysville, Kentucky. There we met Jerry Gore, our tour guide and curator for the entire trip, who also owned a museum.

On Monday, July 10th, we toured numerous historic sites in Maysville, including the Harriet Beecher Stowe Slavery and Freedom Museum, the Paxton Inn, where slaves were placed in covered wagons, the John Parker House which helped 1000 slaves across the Ohio River, and drove down Sutton Street, where slaves were marched down to the river in 1831.

In Ripley, Ohio we saw the John Rankin House, sitting high on a hill above the Ohio River, where thousands of refugees were fed clothed and sheltered. The home was known as "Liberty Hill." In Cincinnati, Ohio, we toured the Underground Railroad Museum and sat in a "Slave Pen." We toured several historic sites and learned that according to the 1830s census, in Louisiana, South Carolina, Maryland, and Virginia, free Blacks owned over 70,000 slaves. There were also White slaves.

Tuesday, July 11th, we visited Wilberforce University and several UGRR sites which included the Presbyterian Church and the Lieut. Col. Charles Young house. Col. Young, a West Point graduate, was America's leading Black soldier prior to WWI. He spoke seven languages and was a veteran of the Spanish-American War. The house reportedly had a tunnel under the road leading from the creek. Runaways hid in the cellar and barn.

Martin Delaney, a Major in the US Army appointed by Abraham Lincoln, attended Harvard Medical School and was the highest-ranking Black in the Union Army. He was the Father of Black Nationalism "before Malcolm X or Dr. Martin Luther King."

In addition to visiting Wilberforce University, founded by the AME Church, the first Black-owned and Black-led College in America, we also toured the National Afro-American Museum and Cultural Center. This is a premier facility on African American life between 1945 and 1965.

We drove to Detroit and Dearborn, Michigan, crossing the longest suspension bridge between two counties in the United States.

Wednesday, July 12th, we toured the Motown "Hitsville, USA" Museum, and the Charles H. Wright Museum of African American History, which houses the largest collection in the world. "AND STILL, WE RISE" chronicles history from more than 3.5 million years ago to modern Detroit. It chronicles GREAT CIVILIZATIONS OF MANKIND, TROUBLE ON THE HORIZON, and TIMELINES OF CAPTURE AND ENSLAVEMENT. The displays included the simulation of a slave ship with life-size mannequins, to represent slaves, lying on the ship, complete with the sound effects of chain, moans, groans, and cries of the slaves. My granddaughter, Imani, and some other participants were unable to complete the tour because of the graphic, realistic displays. However, these were the actual conditions that our ancestors had to endure, and the true history should be displayed. Following a visit to the Henry Ford Museum and Greenfield Village we crossed the US-Canadian border and spent the night in Windsor, Canada.

Thursday, July 13th, we toured the John Freeman Walls Historic Site and Underground Railroad Museum. A fugitive slave from North Carolina, John Freeman Walls, built on land purchased from the Refugee Home Society in 1846. The cabin served as a UGRR railroad terminal. Members of our tour party engaged in a walking trail through the underbrush, crossing a bridge to symbolize an escape to freedom. Our "FOOTSTEPS TO FREEDOM" tour group followed pieces of red cloth through the forest and each person rang a bell as we began the journey. Over 30 families settled in that area of Buxton. One of the Walls children, Earl Walls, was the heavyweight champion of Canada and ranked number three in the world. We visited Buxton, Dresden, and Ontario, Canada, and toured the Uncle Tom's Cabin Historic Site.

In the 1830's, Rev. Josiah Henson and other abolitionists provided refugees with education and skills to become self-sufficient in Upper Canada. In 1841, Henson and allies purchased 200 acres of land and established the British American Institute, one of the first vocational schools in Canada. He was also one of the first Black men to establish and own a church in Canada.

Friday, July 14th, we left Windsor Canada, and crossed the US-Canadian border into Detroit. We left the Detroit airport at 10:30 A.M. for California, arriving at the Ontario airport at 6:10 P.M.

"FOOTSTEPS TO FREEDOM" WAS AN UNFORGETTABLE EXPERIENCE.

I was very cognizant of my Underground Railroad experience as I sang the Star-Spangled Banner at the professional baseball game at the Stadium of the 66ers Minor-League Baseball game on Sunday, September 3. I attended the swearing-in ceremony and reception for first African American Assemblymember to California 62nd District, Assemblymember Wilmer Amina Carter where I also was cognizant of my Underground Railroad experience. The ceremony was held in Sacramento on Monday, December 4, 2006.

2007

I was a recipient of the Visionary Award on February 22nd. TV appearances included an interview on the Local Edition of CNN Time Warner TV Cable. The TV interview by Anchor Leslie Layton took place on Friday, August 24.

There have been numerous awards and recognitions. Notable was the "DREAMERS, VISIONARIES, AND LEADERS" Award in 2016. The brainchild of "DREAMERS, VISIONARIES, AND LEADERS" DVL Founder Regina Weatherspoon-Bell, and in conjunction with the DAILY PRESS NEWSPAPER, the award recognizes "EXTRAORDINARY HIGH DESERT CITIZENS." I was a "LIFETIME ACHIEVEMENT HONOREE." Citations were received for that event from the U.S. House of Representatives and read unto the Congressional Record, the State of California State Senate, County of San Bernardino, the Cities of Victorville, Hesperia, and Adelanto, the Town of Apple Valley, San Bernardino City Unified School District. Numerous awards, certificates, honors, and recognitions have been received for various other events.

Recognitions have been widespread and, additionally, we have had many interesting and well-known speakers come to the PAL Center. In 2008, Mr. James Ramos, Leader of the San Manuel Band of Mission Indians, and Chairman of the San Bernardino County Board of Supervisors, opened his interesting presentation with the singing of the bird dance. Supervisor Josie Gonzales, of the Fifth Supervisorial District, has been a keynote speaker, and she frequently shared and motivated graduates at PAL commencement exercises. Numerous local, national, and internationally known speakers have shared their experiences with graduates at PAL Center and Charter Academy commencements.

<u>2009</u>

A memorable trip for this year was to the 56th Presidential Inauguration of the 44th President of the United States of America - President Barack Hussein Obama. After numerous inquiries, I received a letter dated December 19, 2000, from California Congressman Jerry Lewis stating: "I AM PLEASED TO INFORM YOU THAT MY OFFICE WILL BE ABLE TO PROVIDE YOU WITH TWO TICKETS TO THE 2009 PRESIDENTIAL INAUGURATION." I was thrilled because I had been seeking those hard-to-obtain tickets. My daughter Alvia came from Texas, and my co-worker at the PAL Center, Jacqueline White, went with the group to the inauguration.

We flew from Ontario Airport to Dulles International Airport in Washington D.C., where we boarded a beautiful motorcoach for the Hampton Inn Conference Center in Winchester, Virginia. This was our headquarters as it was absolutely impossible to obtain housing in Washington, D.C., and the immediate area.

Monday morning, we went to Washington and stood in long lines to pick up tickets from various politicians. I picked up invitations and tickets from Congressman Jerry Lewis' office in the Rayburn building. We also toured some sites in Washington, such as the Smithsonian buildings, the Frederick Douglass House and Museum, and other historical sites.

Tuesday morning at 4 AM, the group had continental breakfast at the hotel and boarded the motorcoach for Washington D.C. to join TWO MILLION other inauguration participants. What a day! On the airplanes, in the airports, and all along the journey, we met people from around the world headed for the inauguration.

On Inauguration Day, people were dressed in various ethnic clothing and were ingenious in their efforts to dress for warmth on that extremely cold day. It had snowed the night before, adding to the rigid weather. My daughter Alvia wore my mother's coat to the inauguration so that three Rodgers-Dalton generations participated in the inauguration festivities. It was the same coat that I wore to President Bill Clinton's inauguration, which I attended on January 20, 1993.

I stood on the grounds of the United States Capitol, built by Black slaves, and witnessed the swearing-in of Barack Obama, a Black man, as President of the United States! What a day! My father, who served in the U.S. Army in World War I, and my brother who served in World War II to defend this country stood with me, in spirited memories, on those grounds.

The two million participants at President Obama's inauguration were absolutely thrilled to be part of such a momentous occasion. After the inauguration, as parties were held around the city, we held a celebration party at the Hampton Conference Center. The next morning it was back to Dulles airport and home to California. Witnesses to the inauguration of the first African American President of these United States of America will have the occasion permanently emblazoned in their memories.

These unforgettable experiences made me more acutely aware of the need to educate the populace, and I realized that education must be brought to the people and made accessible where they reside.

XXVII

PAL CHARTER ACADEMY: A REMARKABLE FIRST

The PAL Center was organized and began providing community-based educational services in the mid-1980s and 1990s. Under auspices of local unified school districts, we awarded high school diplomas and GED certificates and services to the nearby Job Corps participants, and to other individuals who enrolled at the PAL Center. Our first high school program was a partnership with Washington High School in the Colton Unified School District. Later we developed a partnership with Citrus High School in the Fontana Unified School District. Our first female adult graduated from Citrus High School with the class of 1991.

From Fontana, we developed a program with the Snowline Unified School District in Victorville, California. We graduated students through the Eagle Summit Academy High School. Administrators from Snowline attended graduation exercises on the PAL Muscoy campus to present the diplomas. One day Snowline Superintendent, Dr. Eric Johnston, called Lawrence and me into his office to inform that the district was re-formatting their educational service model. Tomorrow would be a new day – a new system. It was then that I heard about charter schools.

After hearing details of how the system would work, we decided to discontinue the partnership with the Snowline

District, research the charter school movement, and apply for a charter school of our own through the San Bernardino City Unified School District (SBCUSD). After studying the operations of several schools, we wrote a proposal to petition the SBCUSD for a PAL Charter Academy High School. We met several times with Assistant Superintendent, Dr. Narcisco Cardona, who worked with us and gave suggestions. The Formation Committee consisted of the Honorable Mervyn Dynmally, United States Congressman; Mildred Dalton Hampton-Henry, Ph.D., PESI Founder, and CEO; Clifford Young, Ph.D., Special Assistant to California State University San Bernardino President, Dr. Albert Karnig; Frank Guzman, JD, Attorney-at-Law; Stan Charzn, Contractor, Retired Vice President of Support Services, Community Hospital of San Bernardino; Belva Holder, Retired Teacher, SBCUSD; Rev. Joshua Beckley, Pastor, Ecclesia Christian Fellowship; and Bobby Grizzle, District Sales Manager, Boise Cascade Corporation. The proposal was submitted "by the Formation Committee in cooperation with parents, teachers, community leaders, and other concerned citizens of San Bernardino."

In 2000, Provisional Educational Services, Incorporated (PESI) applied to the San Bernardino City Unified School District (SBCUSD) and was approved to become the first charter school to be approved by The District. The night that the proposal was submitted, I was completely surprised when Dr. Albert Karnig, President of California State University San Bernardino, entered the meeting and came to the front, sat beside me, and spoke on our behalf. I have no doubt that his presence was an asset to our quest for approval.

The charter for The PAL Charter Academy High School, which has repeatedly been renewed by the San Bernardino City Unified School District, and repeatedly approved by WASC (Western Association of Schools and Colleges). recently expanded to include a middle school and additional sites. We have been accepted into the California Interscholastic Federation (CIF), developed championship sports programs, and PAL continues to make great strides. In competition with schools in big districts like San Bernardino, Rialto, Moreno Valley, and Redlands, our determined male athletes won the Basketball 2017 Inland Empire Continuation Athletic League Championship. Both men and women advanced to the semifinals in 2007, and the ladies won the Championship in 2007.

PAL began in 1985 with a community-based elementary school tutoring program and blossomed in 2020 to offer multiple pathways to college and career readiness success. Accredited programs include 6-8th grade middle school and 9-12th grade high school curriculums. Our Upward Bound college-bound program places students into college and on the next rung of their ladder to success. Through several campus programs, participants can simultaneously enroll in college preparation, such as Upward Bound, enroll in vocational skill training, take simultaneous college credits at the local community college, while in high school, receive scholarships, receive legislative leadership training, and partake of individualized study on-line programs. At the PAL Academy, students receive "EDUCATION WITH AN INDIVIDUALIZED APPROACH."

Interestingly, while visiting a PAL Academy sixth-grade classroom, I met a student who had just graduated from Henry Elementary School. It is quite rewarding to think that I have provided pathways and impacted the lives of students from elementary school through college.

In addition to the community-based education focus, the PAL Center has always serviced other community needs. For instance, during the Coronavirus 19 Pandemic, the PAL Center and Academy served 1500 drive-through Grab and Go Meals per day at 3 locations. The Center also serves as a community meeting place.

While on this remarkable journey, I have been blessed to be a number of "firsts." After earning my Ph.D. at Southern Illinois University Carbondale, I was hired as the first middle school counselor for the Watson Chapel School District in Arkansas. My program was so successful that I was asked by the Jefferson County Superintendent of Education, Dr. Turner, to write an article. My first publication was entitled "SETTING UP A RESPONSIVE GUIDANCE PROGRAM IN A MIDDLE SCHOOL." It was published in THE GUIDANCE CLINIC, PARKER PUBLISHING COMPANY.

Subsequent publications included "BLACK RE-ENTRY FEMALES: THEIR CONCERNS AND NEEDS," JOURNAL OF THE NATIONAL ASSOCIATION FOR WOMEN DEANS, ADMINISTRATORS, AND COUNSELORS. VOLUME 48, NO. 4, WASHINGTON D. C., and "THE RESOURCE STUDENT: A COPOUT OR A CHALLENGE." A Dropout Combatant. Empowerment for Change, African Methodist Church, Atlanta, Georgia.

I have received numerous awards. Of the more than 80 awards received, some of the more widely circulated national and international special recognitions include:

- The World's Who's Who of Women, DISTINGUISHED ACHIEVEMENT. 9th Edition of Biographies. February 1987. Cambridge England.
- The International Who's Who of Professional and Business and Women. 2003.
- The American Biographical Institute - DISTINGUISHED LEADERSHIP and PERSONALITIES OF AMERICA; 4th Edition, The United States Congress. SPECIAL CONGRESSIONAL RECOGNITION. 1991, 2005, and 2011.
- The National Association for Equal Opportunity in Higher Education. DISTINGUISHED ALUMNA. 1995.
- National Association for the Advancement of Colored People. WOMAN OF DISTINCTION. 1994.

Numerous recognitions have been received from the State of California Senate, California State Assembly, California Legislature Assembly, and the State of Arkansas.

Awards were received from the County of San Bernardino, and the cities of San Bernardino, Fontana, Apple Valley, Hesperia, Adelanto, and Victorville. Also, I am the recipient of recognition from numerous churches, sororities, fraternities, and civic and community organizations.

Retirement

California State University
In 1995, after 12 years of teaching "on the hill," while providing community-based educational and employment services "in the Valley," and after having proved the vital importance of community-based education, and having won my promotion to FULL professor, I decided to retire from CSUSB.

A retirement celebration was planned by the University and community friends to be held at California State University San Bernardino. The coordinator for the affair was PAL Center Public Relations employee, Lea Cash. Attendees included University personnel, St. Paul AME Church affiliates, Mayor of San Bernardino, Judith Valles, PAL Center staff, students, and friends, and other community supporters.

Entertainment included a dance group of community youth, some of whom were on a college campus for the first time. I was very pleasantly surprised to see my son, Delano Hampton, who came from Minneapolis,

Minnesota to share the event with me. The delicious lunch was prepared by CSUSB personnel.

PAL Center and PAL Academy

After retiring from CSUSB in 1995, I continued to work at the PAL Center as CEO until 2014. I felt the need to guide the organization through many changes that were taking place. Educational designs were changing, charter schools were surfacing, vocational training was taking on greater significance, and societal issues such as homelessness was taking prominence. However, 14 years after retiring from CSUSB, it was time to pass the torch. With my retirement announcement to the PESI Board of Directors, a design and was put in place to select a new CEO. The PESI Corporate Board selected a committee to draw up the design, collect resumes, and interview prospects.

A committee was formed to plan a community-based retirement celebration honoring Dr. Mildred Dalton-Hampton Henry, the retiring CEO. I knew nothing about the arrangements or who was involved. As time progressed, I was told that the retirement celebration would be held on April 17, 2014, and the celebration would be held at the Elks Lodge on the Hill. My only involvement was to submit a supplemental list of individuals to be invited.

On April 17th, I was escorted inside the entrance of the building to be seated and greet arriving guests. I was presented with several floral bouquets and a unique feature was a rocking chair for arriving guests to sign. It now sits in my living room. For the program, I was escorted into The Grand Room, a large banquet room that was tastefully decorated in an African motif. I placed at the Queen's Table which was beautifully decorated by PAL Center employee Jacqueline White and the committee. Dr. Albert Karnig, President of California State University San Bernardino, who was the speaker, was seated next to me.

Other highlights included a saxophone serenade by recording artist "J" Boykin; a creative pantomime dance, "Praise Is What I Do" by Calvin Holder; and commendations and presentations by numerous politicians, organizations, and individuals. The Mistress of Ceremonies, Professor Kathryn Ervin, and the musicians were members of my home church, St. Paul AME Church. Interestingly, I was completely unaware of the African motif decorations, however, I wore a dress brought from Ghana, West Africa. The material was selected, and the dress was made for me as a gift from Chief Kofi Addo. It is one of a kind.

Both retirement celebrations were absolutely marvelous and appreciated!

Words are inadequate to express my gratitude to the PAL Center staff, associates, and friends.

XXVIII

THE TORCH IS PASSED

In 2014, I retired from the PAL Center. The PESI Corporate Board chose Dwaine Radden, Sr., Chief Operating Officer, to pick up the mantle and carry the legacy forward.

The PAL Center thrives under the leadership of Dwaine Radden, Sr. The PAL Charter Academy acquired a second charter school campus in San Bernardino, which offered the same curriculum as the Muscoy campus. Middle school grades six through eight were added on both WASC Accredited PAL Charter Academy campuses. Sports programs offered at the Academy include football, basketball, soccer, softball, and volleyball. The PAL Academy sports program was approved by the California Intramural Federation (CIF), and the football team ended their first complete season with a 7-1 winning record. The men's Mighty Bulls basketball team were the league champions for that same year. The Lady Bulls basketball team were the champions for 2007, and we continue to produce winning athletes as well as academic scholars.

Mr. Radden's business knowledge and background has been a tremendous asset. In addition to being the owner, head coach, and manager of a nationally recognized semi-pro football team, the San Bernardino Raiders, he also owned and operated a new and used appliance business in San Bernardino. His knowledge was invaluable for the survival of the PESI-PAL organization.

During the 28 years that I was CEO, there were times of financial crises when I loaned personal money to keep the organization afloat and meet financial obligations. When Mr. Radden assumed the position as my assistant, knowing the status of the organization, he asked, "DO YOU WANT TO FLY OR DIE?" I answered, "I WANT TO FLY" to which he replied, "THEN LET'S GET TO WORK." We went to work. Finances were stabilized, I retired, my loans to the organization have been repaid, other obligations have been satisfied, and the organization has expanded under his leadership.

While coaching at all levels, little league, high school, or professional football, Radden taught and required participants to repeat and adhere to a life code, whether on or off the field — "The Three "Ds": Discipline + Determination + Dedication = Winner." He also refers to this as "D to the third power." Coach Radden produced winning teams at all levels. He is determined to see that The PAL legacy continues. His roots of commitment have deep roots. His mother, whom he dearly loved, died when he was 12 years old. During her lifetime, however, she instilled a valued code of ethics that he has imparted to others during his lifetime. At age 12, the son wrote a moving poem to his beloved deceased mother.

"ROSES BLOOM THEN SOMEHOW DIE
JUST LIKE THE LOVE OF YOU AND I
ALTHOUGH THE ROSE IS DEAD AND GONE

THE SWEET BUT SIMPLE FRAGRANCE WILL FOREVER LINGER ON."

XXIX

BREAKING NEW GROUND

This Arkansas farm girl had risen from the ashes of a burned-out farm, racism, and denied education, to the pinnacle of university teaching and learning, and helping other disenfranchised individuals attain lofty goals.

Given my cultural background, I felt it important that my colleagues at the University on "The Hill" were familiar with the community in "The Valley," the source of most of our students. When I took colleagues to lunch, I took them to Bobby Ray's Barbecue on the corner of Medical Center Drive and Baseline Avenue in San Bernardino. Mr. Bobby Ray Henderson, I later learned, was somewhat of a neighborhood mayor - knowledgeable, well-versed, and active in community activities; besides, he had the best barbecue in town. Years later, I also learned that Bobby Ray was on the committee that named a new elementary school after me. Expressing my thanks to School Board Member, Danny Tillman, he informed me that Bobby Ray was his representative on the committee that submitted my name and was responsible for the passage of the resolution to name the school on the corner of Mount Vernon Avenue and 14th Street the Dr. Mildred Dalton Henry Elementary school. "One never knows does one" quoted my mother.

Imani called, "Grandma, I received a letter about the groundbreaking of a new school, the Dr. Mildred Dalton Henry Elementary school, named after my grandmother." I said, "Yes, I asked to have the letter sent to you for your family history." Imani replied, "But I want to come. Dad and I talked it over. Can someone meet me?" Of course, we could meet this beautiful youngest grandchild who wanted to personally be a part of this history-making event.

Granddaughter Imani Cheryse Ross, who traveled from Cedar Hills, Texas, joined granddaughter Auvria Hampton, who came from Santa Cruz, California, and Timetra Hampton, who drove from San Diego, California to participate in the groundbreaking ceremonies. The grandchildren were there!

Thursday, August 23, 2012, began with the deep orange sun rising over the mountains in the northeastern sky of Oak Hills, California. Imani shared the anticipation of the day: "Grandma, aren't you excited?" We dressed for the occasion and Imani looked so good and mature in her black pants, white blouse, adorned with jewelry, and black leather heels. My dark blue checkered pleated skirt, topped with a matching dark blue top trimmed with white piping and white and gold buttons, and a blouse kerchief to match the skirt, was hastily draped on my body, and away we went. It was such a joy to be chauffeured by the youngest of my grandchildren. Imani supplied my driving needs during her entire stay, from Wednesday to Sunday.

The groundbreaking ceremony was an affair to remember. At the ceremony, School Board Member Tillman mentioned the fact that Mr. Henderson was in attendance and that he would not be there had he not strongly felt that this honor was justified and deserved. Realizing that Bobby Ray is a quiet behind-the-scenes worker, I was reminded of another saying of our parents, "Things done in the dark will come to light." Sixth Ward San Bernardino City Council Member, Rikke Van Johnson, added to the significance of the location by noting that the school is located on old Route 66 which was popularized in song by famous musician Nat King Cole.

A cross-section of people of all ages and professions, students, children, parents, friends, all attended the groundbreaking ceremonies. From the singers and performers, participating from Roosevelt Elementary School, to my 92-year-old St. Paul AME Church member who said, "If I can walk, I will be there." She was there before I arrived. Mrs. Thelma Earl also brought her husband, for whom she was the caretaker.

<u>Mildred Dalton Henry Elementary School.</u> I had been approached at the PAL Center by colleague George Lee who asked if he could submit my name to the San Bernardino City Unified School District who was seeking names for new schools. I said, "ABSOLUTELY NOT, I DO NOT LIKE POLITICS." Mr. Lee ignored my remarks and collected and submitted the necessary recommendations and requirements.

On August 23rd, 2012, The San Bernardino City Unified School District Board of Education held the groundbreaking ceremony for the new Dr. Mildred Dalton Henry Elementary School. The school is located on Mount Vernon Street, on the Historic Route 66 which was popularized by the legendary singer Nat King Cole. The grand opening celebration for The Dr. Mildred Dalton Henry Elementary School, 1250 W. 14th St., San Bernardino, Home of the Trailblazers, was held October 29, 2013, at 9:30 AM.

At the official grand opening celebration, music was provided by the marching band of Arroyo Valley High School of the San Bernardino City Unified School District, and a time capsule was planted on the campus. Many neighbors and friends attended, including Dr. Albert Karnig, retired President of California State University San Bernardino. People ask me why a school is named after me. I answer that I honestly do not know. I have always been assertive, one might even call me a maverick, and dedicated to helping others achieve their potential.

I was thrilled with the young African American male chosen to take the helm of the new school. Dr. Marcus Funchess set expectations that would make the youngsters leaders. The youth were called "scholars" rather than students. They repeatedly recited self-fulfilling affirmations such as "We are smart, intelligent, full of greatness, and on our way to college." With Dr. Funchess at the helm, I felt my namesake school was in good hands.

I am thrilled each time I attend a function on the campus, when I hear the music department, and when I see the cheerleaders perform on campus and in parades. The seeds planted in Arkansas are harvested in California.

We must not forget our history. This is why, at 85 years old, I "took a knee" at the singing of the Star-Spangled Banner to support of Colin Kaepernick and the young men on the professional football field who chose to kneel to stand up for the right to dignity. It was my "on the spot" decision. Thankfully, Mr. Radden saw my protest action and came to help me to my feet.

Unexpected Champions

Throughout this journey of a lifetime, there has been unexpected support and champions along the way. An unexpected source was responsible for me obtaining my Master's degree. In 1974, stepfather Ben Gates was ill, and Mother was not too well. When I visited them during the Easter vacation, I decided to spend the summer in St. Louis to lend a hand. Several universities were in town, including the University of Missouri, consequently, I saw this as an opportunity to go to summer school and work on a Master's degree. Lawrence had gone with me to St. Louis, and we were to leave Sunday morning returning to Pine Bluff. I visited the University of Missouri at the St. Louis campus and was very unimpressed with the setting and school personnel.

My sister Vhaness told me of a school, just over the state line in Illinois, that her friend attended. We drove over, I loved the campus so much that I left an application under the door of the admissions office on Sunday afternoon. Monday morning, I was there to pick my application up off the floor. In order to attend, however, I needed funds and began seeking financial aid.

When I entered one office and saw a big African American male sitting behind a big desk, I had a feeling that "This is it. I will get help here." It so happens this gentleman knew and had attended Lincoln University with one of my Merrill High School schoolmates, Dr. Grace Wiley. He not only offered me a scholarship for the summer but also a tuition waiver for the following year. I accepted both with glee. With that scholarship in hand, staying in my parents home, and substitute teaching in the Wellston School District, I was successful in funding and obtaining my Master's degree in Educational Counseling from Southern Illinois University at Edwardsville in 1976.

Another incident of cultural relativity was when I was seeking to untangle some problems with one of the PAL Center programs in Sacramento with the California State Department of Education. When I went into one office the person that came out and invited me in to discuss the issue was an African American male with a personality that, when he came to the door, said "This is it." I knew I had found the right person. Again, I felt the sensitivity and knew that we would work it out. Lee Sykes became a staunch supporter of the PAL Center programs and our community-based efforts.

Militancy has its place among self-respecting people. My mother always stood for her principles. This is why during the 2016 Presidential Election I read the headlines of the newspaper in total disbelief! Some professed leaders in the Black Lives Matter (BLM) movement reportedly said "I ain't voting until Black Lives Matter." I felt that supporters on the "I ain't voting" cognitive dissonance trampled on my mother's grave. In the opinion section of the DAILY PRESS NEWSPAPER of August 15, 2016, I expressed "WHY I AM VOTING IN NOVEMBER."

The right to vote is a hard-earned privilege. It was paid for with blood, sweat, tears, and lives. In Arkansas, my mother was told she would lose her teaching job if she joined the NAACP and conducted a voter registration drive. Mother said, "God gave me this job, He will give me another one." She joined the NAACP, became a lifetime member, and conducted a registration drive. She did not lose her job and the family survived. I proclaimed that I WILL vote, and I urge every eligible voter to become adequately informed, vote, and don't forget the bridges that brought us over!

We were taught to be self-respecting individuals. We had to memorize a poem entitled "MYSELF" by an unknown author in BOWLES STAR POEM BOOK NO. 3. Excerpts read, in part:

I HAVE TO LIVE WITH MYSELF, AND SO I WOULD BE FIT FOR MYSELF TO KNOW; I WANT TO BE ABLE AS THE DAYS GO BY ALWAYS TO LOOK MYSELF STRAIGHT IN THE EYE.

I WANT TO GO OUT WITH MY HEAD ERECT, I WANT TO DESERVE THE WORLD'S RESPECT.

I NEVER CAN HIDE MYSELF FROM ME, I SEE WHAT OTHERS MAY NEVER SEE.

I KNOW WHAT OTHERS MAY NEVER KNOW. I CAN NEVER FOOL MYSELF, AND SO

WHATEVER MAY HAPPEN I WANT TO BE SELF-RESPECTING AND CONSCIENCE-FREE.

XXX

DON'T TREAD ON ME

"Keep your head on a swivel" is a saying frequently uttered. The ending of 2017 and the beginning of 2018 was filled with unanticipated excitement. It not only ended with the dropping of the New Year's Eve ball in New York City, but I found that an unexpected ball was about to be dropped on the PAL Center in San Bernardino. I was spending the Christmas holidays with daughter Alvia Hampton Turner Page and her family in Fort Worth, Texas, returning to California on December 30, 2017. On December 29th, during a phone call, I was informed that there were plans to move another charter school, grades K-8, onto the campus that we were currently renting from First Church of the Nazarene in San Bernardino.

We had previously been asked to assume the site and student body of another charter high school whose charter was being revoked by the San Bernardino City Unified School District. We accepted the challenge, spent approximately $50,000 building walls, rooms, placing banners, re-apportioning, acquiring personnel, and building a very inviting campus for our staff and new student body. We constructed order out of chaos, and now a bombshell was dropped that we would share campus facilities with another school. Neither the Provisional Educational Services Incorporated (PESI) CEO, the PESI Corporate Board, the PAL Charter Academy High

School Board of Advisors, or any PAL stakeholders had been consulted.

When we heard, by way of "the grapevine", that the move was to take place, we were informed that it was a "done deal." My reply was "like heck it is." We would not be ignored and treated in such a disrespectful, unprofessional manner. Having been through the abhorrent conditions of the segregated and unequal South, I immediately thought of the unfair tactics of segregation when African Americans were too often treated as voiceless non-persons. However, this is a new day and we have paid an astronomical price for respect, equity, and fairness. This disrespect was not acceptable and would not be tolerated.

Mr. Dwaine Radden, CEO, and I went to work and demanded our right for inclusion, and to fight against what would have been an unfair logistical and legal nightmare. I contacted the San Bernardino City Unified School District (SBCUSD) Board of Education members, who were unaware of the planned takeover; the SBCUSD Superintendent; the Director of Charter Schools; and PESI and PAL Advisory Board Members. Meanwhile, Mr. Radden contacted the Director of Charter Schools, the church representatives, and other pertinent individuals, to express our dissatisfaction, our refusal to be excluded, and our intent to fight for the right. Mr. Radden presented Mr. Tickell, Charter School Director, with possible alternative sites for the Casa Ramona Academy. Research also revealed that our PAL Charter High School was an alternative school, an Alternative Schools Accountability Model school, which could not mix elementary and high school students on the same campus. This was a State of California education code.

The Director of Charter Schools withdrew his endorsement of the merger; the church withdrew its offer to rent to the school who had arranged a "done deal" without our knowledge, and a nightmare was averted. So-called "done deals" can be undone, if improperly devised. Our immediate attention and determination demonstrated the saying "don't tread on me," which is displayed on the flag with the coiled snake. A colloquial statement of years past was "Get back, Jack!"

The Earthquake That Shook America

An earth-shaking event happened in the year 2016. There was no warning, and the seismograph did not measure the earthquake that occurred on November 8, 2016. However, the upheaval was felt along the fault lines all across America, from coast to coast. The election of 2016 will go down in history as one of a kind. It was a very hotly contested, contemptuous, presidential election, with accusations, innuendos, verbal attacks, and uncivilized behavior.

The match between Republican Donald Trump and Democrat Secretary of State Hillary Clinton had been bitterly fought. Monday night before the election, most indications were that Hillary Clinton would win. There were very long lines of voters all across the country. Tuesday, as the polls closed, and results began to pour in, shock occurred across the nation. State after state-reported victories for Donald Trump. My heart sank. When it appeared that Donald Trump may become the President-Elect, I turned off the TV. I was absolutely sick and angry that Hillary Clinton supporters did not go to the polls in sufficient numbers to place her in the winner's column. However, it was later reported that there was Russian interference in our electoral process which was thought to have altered the results. Hillary Clinton actually did win the popular vote. It was the electoral college that put Donald Trump into office as the 45th President of the United States.

Trump had attacked Hillary Clinton calling her "Crooked Hillary," "Liar Hillary," said she was a criminal, and he would have her arrested, and made all kinds of crazy, insulting remarks. This lady had devoted 30+ years of her life to the country, including being First Lady, when husband Bill Clinton was President, to being Secretary of State, representing this country around the world. Donald Trump, who had been so uncouth and insulting, never served his country, and who had never spent a day in political office, was being voted into the Presidency? Unbelievable!

This man who said he would build a wall to keep Mexicans from entering the United States; who would refuse to admit Muslims to the country; who claimed President

Obama was not born in the United States and should be impeached; who had insulted and attacked numerous women; THIS man was being elected President of these United States of America??

Unbelievable!

His blind supporters, racists, and hate-mongers, apparently all came out of the woodwork. There were also questions of incidents that may have interfered with the election. Intimidation had been widely encouraged by Trump, telling his supporters to go to the polls on election day and watch, even carry their weapons. This was obviously designed to intimidate.

Results that showed Trump as the winner, led to comments such as "this is the day that America died." Voters said, "America chose hate over hope." "We chose the dark side over light." The voting public in the United States chose Donald Trump to be the next President of the United States of America. Canada's immigration site crashed because so many people wanted to move north to Canada and leave the United States. I did not watch the final results, and every time Trump's face or anything about him came on the TV screen, I changed the channel. I watched Family Feud until I drifted off to sleep.

The next day, Wednesday, I prepared to interview President Albert Karnig, retired President of California State University San Bernardino, at his home in San Bernardino. Late that evening, I saw on TV that students from various campuses across the country were protesting and marching in the streets chanting "Trump is not my President," among other things. Thursday, as the protests continued and became bigger, I felt anger and anguish that President Barack Obama was subjected to sitting in the same room with Donald Trump, the man who had unmercifully insulted the President. The two met to publicly discuss passing the reins of the Presidency from Obama to Trump. How ironic! My heart bled for President Obama, who graciously fulfilled the role. It was too painful to look at the television.

The protests in the streets continued and enlarged. Later, on TV, I viewed two large groups of people in Los Angeles, both seemingly marching toward City Hall. Earlier, a group of marchers shut down a major freeway. Thousands were in the streets.

The third day of protests highlighted groups in Portland, Oregon where police called the protests full-scale "riots," with cars set afire, buildings damaged, and out-of-control behaviors. The media noted that the South Carolina Ku Klux Klan had called for rallies "now that they have won," flyers were circulating in Texas calling for "tar and feathering" individuals, and vigilantes were springing up, as feared. Unprecedented violence is taking place daily. Worshipers are being slaughtered in churches and synagogues, along with street violence. Hate, which at one time hid behind sheets and hoods, was now out in the open with suits, uniforms, and guns. The unfounded divisive accusations and rhetoric between the political parties is tearing the country apart. The Saga of The Earthquake That Shook America is continuing its earth-shattering consequences.

Insurrection Day in America

After four tumultuous years in office, Republican Donald Trump lost the 2020 Presidential Election to Democratic Vice President Joseph Biden. However, having lost the 2020 Presidential Election, Donald Trump created further turmoil. Monday, January 6, 2021, will go down in history as "a day in infamy." Outgoing President Donald Trump had lost the election to Sen. Joseph Biden, however, Trump refused to accept the election results. He encouraged his followers to come to Washington D.C. "ready for combat," continuingly stating that the election was "stolen" from him. Votes had been recounted in several states and he had lost the argument in every court where he contested the election. He had no documentation to support his claim. Trump especially sought to discount votes in heavily Black populated areas, such as cities like Atlanta and Philadelphia.

Thousands came to Washington where Trump spoke and then urged the crowd to march to the Capitol building. They broke windows, broke open doors, loudly proclaiming that they would destroy, commit violence, and kill Vice President Michael Pence and the Speaker of the House of the Representative, Nancy Pelosi. The news media showed a picture of a rioter seated in Representative Pelosi's chair with his feet on her desk. Rioters roamed through the building ransacking offices, while Congress was still in session to accept the official mandate of the Electoral College, officially certifying that Senators Joseph Biden and Kamela Harris were officially elected President and Vice President of the United States.

Members of Congress were taken by Capitol Police to a safer section of the building. When the Capitol was under siege, police reportedly called the Pentagon for military help. Help was reportedly denied by Charles Flynn, brother of Michael Flynn, an ardent supporter of Donald Trump.

The insurrectionist group roamed through the halls looting, desecrating, and shouting slogans to destroy and kill. Five people lost their lives during the chaos. Participants in this insurrection were proven to be members of White supremacists, Ku Klux Klan, Nazis, and other hate groups. When order was restored, Congress went back to work, working through the night, and certified the votes of the Electoral College.

Because President Donald Trump reportedly instigated the insurrection, impeachment procedures were immediately begun against him by Members of the House of Representatives. This was the first time in history that a "sitting" president would be impeached twice during his four-year term. With the inauguration scheduled for January 20, impeachment procedures continued following the inauguration. When the impeachment trial was held, the House of Representatives voted to impeach the President, however, the Senate, unbelievably, voted to acquit him of the charges. It should be noted that 16 Republican senators voted with the Democratic senators to find Donald Trump guilty as charged.

Another first occurred when President Trump refused to attend the inauguration ceremonies or to transfer power peacefully for incoming President Joe Biden. Instead, Trump retreated to his Mar-a-Lago residence in Miami Florida, leaving Washington the morning of Wednesday, January 20, 2021. This was the first time in over 100 years that an outgoing president refused to participate in the transfer of power. Vice President Michael Pence offered his cooperation for the inaugural activities and participated accordingly.

Three living Presidents attended the ceremony: Presidents William "Bill" Clinton, George W. Bush, and Barack Obama. President Jimmy Carter was physically unable to attend, however, he sent his congratulations. It was a glorious day with many firsts. President Biden was the oldest person to become President of the United States. Vice President Harris was the first female and the first Black and Asian American to be elected Vice President.

Black In America

As I listen to the news, I think of the words singer James Brown said when he was sent to jail, "Ain't nothing changed but the address." There is good and bad everywhere, but unfortunately, too often, the bad supersedes the good. When I was a child, my parents took neighbors to the polls to register and vote. When I became an adult, I drove neighbors to the polls to vote. In

2021 Jim Crow laws are still being introduced to suppress voter registration and voting, designed specifically to disenfranchise Blacks and other minority groups.

I have personally fought racism all of my life. Throughout this road well-traveled, I have experienced or witnessed physical violence, death threats, White privilege, and racial slurs. Being Black in America has too often meant that you are not to be respected or treated as a human being. If a Black man walks through a community, minding their own business, gets shot to death, and the murderer goes free, where is the "liberty and justice for all"? When a Black gain is deemed to be a White loss, where is the "equity"?

When a Black parent is afraid to send a child outside of the home to play, or fears going to the morgue to identify a body because a White man said he "felt threatened," what happened to the "land of the free"? When I watch a Black man slowly murdered on TV by an authority figure and see continued so-called accidental murder of Black males and females, apparently some individuals feel that White people's existence is secured, protected, and rendered sacred. As harsh as this sounds, it is reality. I refuse to tiptoe around the subject of racism because I am Black in America.

RACISM MUST CEASE.

XXXI

A LOOK AHEAD

As the years quickly become history, I wonder where and how I will spend my last years. As I see my peers become incapacitated and observe them in various retirement and healthcare facilities, I began to research these facilities based on several criteria: Location convenient to my children, family, and caretakers who can oversee my treatment; the convenience of the location for visitors, such as family and friends; and, a place where healthcare personnel will be well-qualified, sensitive, and will treat me with compassion, kindness, and dignity as I travel to the end of the road.

What will become of the legacy? Will the younger generations assure that the legacy continues?

Spiritual Intervention

Approximately eight years before retirement, God brought a young man to the PAL Center, and into my life, who became my spiritual son. His mother died when he was 12 years of age, and he has felt the void through the years. Somehow, we felt a spiritual connection and I became his spiritual mother and mentor.

I was in an automobile accident with a man who had two children in his vehicle. I borrowed a cell phone to call the PAL Center. Lawrence was not available, and when told I was in an accident, Dwaine Radden immediately rushed to the site, which I incorrectly identified, to take charge. He calmed my fears and tears, communicated with the police officer, had my car towed, took me to eat and calm down, and rented a car for me before returning to the PAL Center to further regain my composure. Never having experienced such a traumatic incident, I was completely lost, and I felt that this young man was sent by God.

Dwaine calls every morning to be sure that I am "moving and grooving," and to see if I need anything. He had an alarm system installed where I live in the country, oversees my cars and transportation, and locates resources for whatever is needed for my safety and comfort. His parting words each morning are always "Call me if you need me."

Dwaine Radden, Sr. wanted his five children to have a grandmother of his choosing, and the security of knowing that if anything happened to him there was someone, in addition to their mother Melinda, who could continue to instill principles to help them achieve their life goals. It has been most comforting to have God send this young man my way.

XXXII

EPILOGUE

As a child in Arkansas, to be told of living in California conjured up thoughts of living in a mystical fairyland. Visiting family members from California who indicated they would never return to Arkansas to live, increased the mystical perception of California. To become a part of the mystical California scene was a wonderment.

As I approached the beautiful campus of CSUSB, nestled at the foot of the mountains, I thought of the responsibility that I would assume in this new place in my life and history. The feelings of responsibility increased as I attended the first faculty meeting and found that I was the only full-time African American on the faculty in the School of Education at the CSUSB institution. A product of the South, I again felt the responsibility and remembered the words that had been instilled over the years, "you have to be better in order to be considered equal."

I became the first African American to earn the titles of Assistant Professor, Associate Professor, Full Professor and was awarded the ultimate title of Professor Emeritus in the School of Education, by Dr. Albert Karnig. The School of Education was later renamed the College of Education. The friendly face of Dean Ernie Garcia and being introduced as one of his recruits increased my determination to be successful, especially since there had never been a full-time tenured African American professor in the School of Education. Tenure at CSUSB became my goal, against all odds. The main classes assigned to me to teach were Introduction to Counseling, Cross-cultural Counseling, and Fieldwork.

I felt a personal kindred to the cultural class because of my keen awareness of the importance of culture to one's behavior. Knowing that counselors need to relate to their student's environments, I felt a personal responsibility to make culture a key element in their training. As each culture was explored a prominent member of that culture was invited to class to give first-hand experiences. Consequently, Cross-cultural counseling became somewhat of a signature class for my tenure.

In an interview by Dr. Daniel Stewart, which was published in the WISDOM IN EDUCATION, VOL. 6, ISSUE 1, 2016, I stated that:

ALL CULTURES HAVE HIGH AND LOW ACHIEVERS. MOST OF THE TIME THE LOWER ACHIEVERS ARE AT THAT LEVEL DUE TO A LACK OF OPPORTUNITY. TO SEE THE LESSER-ADVANTAGED STUDENTS CROSS THE PAL CENTER STAGE RECEIVING HIGH SCHOOL DIPLOMAS TO THE CHEERING AND ADULATION OF THEIR FAMILIES HAS BEEN MOST REWARDING. ADDITIONALLY, TO HAVE PREPARED AND TRAINED YOUTH FOR EMPLOYMENT AND SEE THEM BECOME SELF-SUPPORTING HAS BEEN OF IMMEASURABLE SATISFACTION.

As for cultural equity in employment, it has been surprising to see that the more things change, the more they remain the same. I was employed at CSUSB over 30 years ago, however, the lack of African Americans promoted in tenure track positions then and now continues to amaze me.

It is rewarding to know, however, that I have positively impacted the lives of many individuals, from babies in the PAL Center's childcare programs, to college graduates at CSUSB, to older citizens who came to the PAL Center and Academy to get their diplomas, GEDs, and English as a Second Language certificates. Sometimes there is a feeling of "mission accomplished," yet I know there is still much to be done.

The Legacy Personified

One never knows the impact their behavior is having on observers. Granddaughter, Auvria (Vera) Hampton, who flies around the country for Student Outreach and Recruitment for California State University, has said on several occasions, "I am going to be just like you Grandmom." Vera has completed her Master's Degree, has enrolled in a Doctoral Program, and desires to become a University Professor. Her sister, Timetra Hampton, is a University of California Associate Director of Students Admission. She travels, recruits, and evaluates admits for the University of California system. Granddaughter, Mizz Turner Jones, teaches music to elementary students in the Houston, Texas school district area. Mizz also plans to seek her Doctorate. Her sister, Misti, taught outdoor survival courses, and art and music to elementary students in a Montessori school in the Fort Worth area. Their mother, my daughter Alvia LaVerne, retired from teaching after 38 years of working "in the trenches" with elementary school children, in Arkansas and Texas. Educational professions and pursuits are definitely a part of the family legacy.

The Heart of the Matter

On April 9, 2019, I received an unsettling phone call from my daughter-in-law, Joyce, informing me that my son, Lawrence, had suffered a major heart attack and was being transported from Kaiser Hospital in Fontana to Saint Bernardine Hospital in San Bernardino. I called Dwaine Radden, who immediately went to the hospital. I headed south, with an anxious heart, and the throttle opened on the automobile. Thankfully, the heart operation on Lawrence was successful, the road to recovery is successful, and Lawrence has returned to teaching tennis, and the tennis court, with no restrictions. We are thankful!

And the Beat Goes On

In July 2019, the Hampton Family - Lawrence, Joyce, Timetra, and Auvria, hosted the Rodgers-Dalton Family reunion in San Diego, California. It was wonderful seeing family from Arkansas, Tennessee, Florida, Texas, Nevada, and California. Likewise, it was great enjoying the fellowship, the history, and the continuing family legacy. This family tradition increased my desire to return to the St. Paul, Minnesota area where I bore five children, worked, and lived for 18 years.

On October 17, 2019, Alvia came from Fort Worth, Texas and we went to St. Paul Minneapolis to visit my son Delano (Del) Hampton, and the St. Paul-Minneapolis area. There were 18 years of family living in that area. Four of the children were born while living in the still existing 848 Fuller Avenue home in St. Paul. Dr. AA Kugler delivered all five babies at St. Joseph Hospital in St. Paul. Seeing Maxfield Elementary School, one block away, and Pilgrim Baptist Church, three blocks away, was nostalgic. We visited several area sites including Ft. Snelling, where son Angelo Jerome, and ex-husband Lawrence Theodis, are buried. We toured St. Paul, Minneapolis, St. Paul Park, Newport, Cottage Grove, Woodbury, St. Thomas Academy (where Angelo attended school), and other sites. It was great to "stroll down memory lane." Alvia especially wanted to visit Paisley Park, the Memorial for Prince, of Purple Rain fame.

Now that Alvia is retired, after 38 years of teaching, she is more readily available to travel. As former teachers, we both commented on the difference in today's educational environment compared to our classroom experiences. Too often, too many students are unruly, and too many parents are a problem. Administrators, who too often have no classroom experiences, are making decisions for educators. Respect for the teaching profession is dwindling. Unfortunately, all of these factors have led to a shortage of teachers and the situation is getting worse.

Black History Honoree

Black History has always been a vital part of my cultural life. Each year I participate in activities, display history, and I am a strong advocate for Black History celebrations. Consequently, I attended the Dr. Mildred Dalton Henry Elementary School Black History celebration on March 5, 2020. I was absolutely astounded to see that I was the main honoree for the celebration, in addition to the traditional historical figures such as Dr. Martin Luther King, Sojourner Truth, Rosa Parks, Dr. Charles Drew, and others. The students and staff at Henry Elementary presented an excellent stage production.

The local SAN BERNARDINO SUN NEWSPAPER headline read, "SAN BERNARDINO ICON HONORED DURING BLACK HISTORY MONTH PERFORMANCE." The newspaper continued, "MORE THAN SIX YEARS AFTER SAN BERNARDINO CITY UNIFIED OPENED AN ELEMENTARY SCHOOL BEARING HER NAME, DR. MILDRED HENRY WAS HONORED FRIDAY AT AN ASSEMBLY CELEBRATING BLACK HISTORY MONTH. THE PRODUCTION INCLUDED POEM READING, SINGING, AFRICAN DANCING, A SKIT, AND ART THAT STAFF MEMBERS AND TEACHERS PROMOTE MORE

AND MORE ON-CAMPUS. HENRY IS A RETIRED CEO AND FOUNDER OF THE PROVISIONAL ACCELERATED LEARNING CENTER IN SAN BERNARDINO'S MUSCOY AREA. HER MOTTO, "DARE TO DO THE IMPOSSIBLE," INSPIRED HER AND HER NONPROFIT'S WORK WITH HUNDREDS OF AT-RISK CHILDREN AND UNDERPRIVILEGED YOUTH. THE ARKANSAS NATIVE AND LONGTIME SAN BERNARDINO RESIDENT WAS NAMED PROFESSOR EMERITUS AT CAL STATE SAN BERNARDINO IN 2006 AND WAS THE FIRST AFRICAN AMERICAN TO BECOME A TENURED PROFESSOR IN THE UNIVERSITY'S COLLEGE OF EDUCATION. "IT'S BEEN MY CALLING - MY MISSION HERE ON THIS EARTH - TO HELP OTHERS, AND NOTHING IS IMPOSSIBLE, SHE TOLD SUN COLUMNIST MICHAEL NOLAN IN A 2014 INTERVIEW."

Parents, staff, and students made the costumes, the excellent stage sets, the art posted around the room, and in general, put on a professional celebration.

Full Circle

In February 2020, I made a full circle. I began my California journey in Fontana in August 1983, and on February 29, 2020, I was honored to be a "Phenomenal Woman" Grand Marshal in the Annual Fontana Black History Parade held in North Fontana. The parade was held in a newer section which, during my Fontana residency, was all open fields. The Ku Klux Klan no longer told us that we could not honor Black Americans. In fact, the Mayor of Fontana is an African American female, Mayor Aquanetta Warren, who is gaining widespread recognition for her effective management.

Family Blessings

I have been blessed to be the mother of five children: Angelo Jerome, Alvia LaVerne, Delano Eugene, Lawrence Terry, and Pamela Jeanne. I am the grandmother of five children: Tory, Mizz, Misti, Timetra, Auvria, and Imani. My great-grandchildren are Tory Jr., Marcus, Johnathan, Maci, and Milani. My three great-great-grandchildren are Liyah, Marcus Jr, and Isa. I am also the spiritual mother of one son: Dwaine Radden, Sr., and five spiritual grandchildren: Terrance, Dwaine Jr., Virginia, Derrick, and DeShawn.

I am thankful.

XXXIII

BEQUEATH

I have been asked how I want people to remember me. Dr. Mary McLeod Bethune, my great educator idol, left her legacy in a LAST WILL AND TESTAMENT. I, too, have principles in which I believe. I bequeath them hoping that my experiences will be of value to someone.

I LEAVE YOU

Love: ~ Love of Self, and Agape Love for your fellow man.

An Obligation to Serve: ~ To help somebody, lift as you climb.

A Duty to Teach: ~ Knowledge is to be shared. I believe that if young African Americans knew of their rich heritage, and the reasons to be proud and love themselves, they would be less likely to engage in negative behaviors.

A Challenge to Keep the Legacies Alive: ~ Know and Teach your history. Pass it to the next generation.

Tenacity and Determination: ~ Never accept "No" as an answer when there is a human need that you can provide.

Peace: ~ If you can do something about a problem, do it. If not, turn it over to a higher power - the Master of all mankind.

Strength: ~ Strength to climb every mountain until you find <u>YOUR</u> dream.

My family's cotton gin, store, and farm were burned in Arkansas, but the dream continued. "Stony the road we trod, bitter the chastening rod," but we "march on 'til victory is won," as James Weldon Johnson inspires in "Lift Every Voice and Sing."

SUCCESS!
From The Ashes I Rose

The Bridge Builder

An old man going a lone highway

Came at the evening, cold and gray

To a chasm vast and deep and wide.

The old man crossed in the twilight dim,

The sullen stream had no fear for him,

But he turned when safe on the other side

And built a bridge to span the tide.

"Old man," said a pilgrim standing near,

"You are wasting your strength building here;

Your journey will end with the ending day.

You never again will pass this way;

You've crossed the chasm deep and wide

Why build you this bridge at evening tide?"

The builder lifted his old gray head –

"Good friend, in the path I have come," he said,

"There followeth after me today

A youth whose feet must pass this way;

This chasm that has been as naught to me

To that fair-haired youth may a pitfall be;

He, too, must cross in the twilight dim;

Good friend, I am building this bridge for him."

Will Allen Dromgoole

As one reflects on the poem above, and watches the simply gorgeous sunrise, as the one this morning, we know why Provisional Educational Services, Inc. was incorporated in December 1984 as a non-profit, 501(c)(3) State of California Corporation and why the DBA, The PAL Center, was organized. What an opportunity, to be Blessed to help youth cross "a chasm vast and deep and wide"!

Dr. Mildred Dalton Hampton-Henry

Sample PAL Graduation Data
"A Journey of a Thousand Miles Begins with a Single Step"

PAL CENTER GRADUATES & SPEAKERS

Year	Number of Graduates			Speaker
	GED	HSD	ABE	
1993	3	21		Jorge Hernandez Attorney
1995	24	5	20	Dr. Arthur Fletcher, U.S. Civil Rights Commissioner "Father of Affirmative Action"
1996				Ronald Johnson Founder, Harlem Institute of Positive Education
1997	37	6		Ms. Jewel Diamond Taylor Author, Motivational Speaker
2000	33	16		Rubin "Hurricane" Carter World Boxing Champion
2001	17	35		Honorable Jerry Eaves, 5th District Supervisor, San Bernardino County
2002	11	9		Honorable Nell Soto, Senator 32nd Senatorial District State of California Theme: "Keep Your Eyes on the Prize"
2003	5	13		Dr. Clifford Young, Assistant to President, Government Relations Director Technology Transfer, Cal State University San Bernardino
2004		17		Dr. Elsa Valdez, Cal State University San Bernardino
2005		34		Dr. Renatta Osterdock, Chief of Neurosurgery Loma Linda Medical School Hospital; Separated twins, CNN Honoree

Year	Number of Graduates			Speaker
	GED	HSD	ABE	
2006		37		Ms. Beverly White TV News Anchor & Reporter Channel 4, Los Angeles Theme: "And Still We Rise"
2007		46		Honorable Josie Gonzales, 5th District Supervisor San Bernardino County Theme: "Education is Not a Gift, But an Achievement"
2008		60		Dr. George McKenna, School Reformer Movie: The George McKenna story, played by Denzel Washington Theme: "The Past is my Heritage. The Present is My Responsibility, The Future is My Challenge"
2009		80		Dr. Darlene Willis, CoFounder Empowering Parents and College Bound. Theme: "If you believe it, you can achieve it!"
2010		65		Dr. Albert Karnig, President California State University, San Bernardino Theme: "If you believe it, you can achieve it!"
2011				Mr. James Ramos, Chairman San Manual Band of Mission California Commission on Education San Bernardino Valley College Trustee
2012		82		Mr. Greg Bell, Former NFL Star Executive, Founder, Athletes for Life, Entrepreneur, Consultant, Broker

Year	Number of Graduates			Speaker
	GED	HSD	ABE	
2013		73		Honorable Aquanetta Warren, Mayor, City of Fontana
2014				Dr. Terrence Roberts One of "The Little Rock Nine"
2015		33		Mr. Mark Hartley Director, Student Leadership & Development California State University San Bernardino Theme: "Nothing is Impossible, The Word Itself says 'I', Possible"
2016				Mr. Ted Alejandra, Superintendent San Bernardino County Schools
2017		38		Mr. Danny Tillman, Member San Bernardino City School District Board of Education
2018				Mr. Reginald Webb, CEO Webb Family Enterprise 16 McDonald Restaurants
2019		60		Mr. James Curtis, JD, Executive Director, NAMI Pomona Valley

CITY AWARDS

City of Fontana. ***Commissioner, Mobile Home Rent Review***. October 17, 1984. Mayor Nathan Simon.

City of San Bernardino. ***1990 Woman of The Year***. 1991. Mayor Bob Holcomb.

City of San Bernardino. ***Services Rendered to San Bernardino City Library Literacy Program***. 1992.

Banning City Unified School District. ***Award***. 1992.

City of San Bernardino. ***Recognition of Dedicated Service***. 1999. Mayor Judith Valles.

City of San Bernardino. ***Recognition of Your 10 Years of Commitment and Outstanding Dedication to the Children of Our Community***. July 18, 2003. Mayor Judy Valles.

City of San Bernardino. ***Certificate of Recognition of Your Contribution to the Black History Parade, Division Marshall***. February 2006. Mayor Judy Valles.

City of Victorville. ***Certificate of Recognition and Appreciation for "Dreamers, Visionaries, and Leaders" DLV Lifetime Achievement Honoree***. February 6, 2016. Mayor Gloria Garcia.

City of Hesperia. ***Certificate of Appreciation "Dreamers,***

Visionaries, and Leaders" DLV Lifetime Achievement Honoree February 6, 2016. Mayor William J. Holland.

City of Adelanto. *Special Recognition Award "Dreamers, Visionaries, and Leaders" DLV Lifetime Achievement Honoree February 6, 2016*. Mayor Richard Kerr.

Town of Apple Valley. *Certificate of Recognition "Dreamers, Visionaries, and Leaders" DLV Lifetime Achievement Honoree February 6, 2016*. Mayor Barb Stanton.

San Bernardino City Unified School District. *Certificate of Recognition.* Superintendent Dr. Dale Marsden and Board President Dr. Margaret Hill.

COUNTY AWARDS

County of San Bernardino. ***1990 Woman of the Year***. 1991. Board of Supervisors.

County of San Bernardino. ***Woman of Distinction Award***. 1999.

County of San Bernardino. ***Certificate of Recognition for Receiving a 2003 Black Rose Award***. September 12, 2003. Supervisor Jerry Eaves 5th District.

San Bernardino County Association of African-American Employees. ***2007 Ebony Visionary Award***. 2007.

County of San Bernardino. ***Certificate of Recognition for Dreamers, Visionaries, and Leaders Lifetime Achievement Honoree***. February 6, 2016. Robert A. Lovingood, 1st District Supervisor.

STATE AWARDS

State of California Legislature. ***Woman of The Year 1990***. 1991.

State of California Senate. ***Recognition of Retirement***. 1999. Senator Joe Baca, 32nd Senatorial District.

California Legislative Assembly. ***Resolution Recognition of Retirement***. 1999.

California Legislative Assembly. ***Certificate of Recognition***. February 8, 2003. Assemblymember John Longville, 62nd District. *"It is a pleasure to take this opportunity to salute you for the many contributions you have made to the City of San Bernardino and to the community at large. You have touched the lives of so many. I extend birthday greetings and best wishes for your continued good health, happiness, and success, on the occasion of your 70th birthday."*

State of California Senate. ***Certificate of Recognition***. September 12, 2003. Senator Nell Soto. 32nd District. *"Congratulations on your selection as a recipient of the '2003 Black Rose Award' the San Bernardino Black Culture Foundation. I commend your dedication and tireless efforts supporting the needs of our students in the Inland Empire. Your spirit of goodwill is treasured in our community."*

State of California. ***Certificate of Recognition***. October 11, 2003. Senator Nell Soto, 32nd District. "A Dream in the Making Awards".

State of California Senate. ***Certificate of Commendation for Excellence in Education***. December 6, 2005. Senator Nell Soto.

State of Arkansas. ***Recognition of Retirement***. 2008.

California State Senate. ***Certificate of Recognition 2011 Community Builder Award Honoree***. December 3, 2011. Senator Gloria Negrete McLeod.

California Legislative Assembly. ***Certificate of Recognition. Outstanding Accomplishments***. December 3, 2011. Assemblymember Wilmer Amina Carter, 62nd Assembly District. Dedicated service to our community.

California State Assembly. ***California Legislature Certificate of Recognition***. March 8, 2013. Assemblymember Mike Morell.

California State Senate. ***Certificate of Recognition. Dreamers, Visionaries, and Leaders Project Lifetime Achievement Honoree***. February 6, 2016. Senator Sharon Runner, 21st Senatorial District.

California State Assembly. ***Certificate of Recognition. 2016 Dreamers, Visionaries, and Leaders Lifetime Achievement Honoree***. February 6, 2016. Assemblymember Jay Obernolte, 33rd Assembly District.

NATIONAL AWARDS

National Association for Equal Opportunity and Higher Education. ***Distinguished Alumni***. March 1985.

United States House of Representatives. ***1990 Woman of the Year***. 1991. Congressman George Brown.

National Association for the Advancement of Colored People. ***Woman of Distinction Award***. 1994.

United States House of Representatives. ***Certificate of Special Congressional Recognition***. December 6, 2005. Congressman Joe Baca, 43rd Congressional District. *"In recognition of your outstanding civic and community leadership. I comment your commitment to enhancing the educational needs of the citizens you serve in the Inland Empire and beyond. Thank you for you loyal and dedicated service to our community and our nation and best wishes in all of your future endeavors."*

United States Congress. ***Certificate of Special Congressional Recognition. Outstanding Valuable Service to the Community***. December 3, 2011.

United States House of Representatives. ***Congressional Record, February 4, 2016 Proceedings and Debates Of The 114th Congress, Second Session***. United States House of Representatives. Recognition read to the Congressional Record, ***Lifetime Achievement Award*** from the **Dreamers,**

Visionaries, and Leaders Project. February 2016. Congressman Paul Cook, California 8th Congressional District.

American Biographical Institute. ***Distinguished Leadership Award***.

American Biographical Institute. ***Personalities of America***, honoring America's leaders. Fourth Edition. Contributions to Public Achievement and Professional Achievement.

INTERNATIONAL AWARDS

The World Who's Who of Women. ***Certificate of Merit for Distinguished Achievement***. 9th edition of Biographies. February 1987. Cambridge England.

International Who's Who of Professional and Business Women. 2003 Honoree.

CIVIC AND COMMUNITY AWARDS

The Atlanta University National Center of Leadership and Development and the United States Office of Education. ***Certificate of Participation***. 1979.

Mexican American Professional Management Association. ***Certificate of Appreciation Recognition of Outstanding Effort as a Member of "Youth Educational and Motivational Program"***. July 11, 1984.

Bethel African Methodist Episcopal Church. ***Certificate of Appreciation for Outstanding Service and Devotion to the Cause***. September 30, 1984.

831st Air Division. ***Award***. 1985.

West San Bernardino Kiwanis Club. ***Certificate of Appreciation***. January 16, 1986. Guest Speaker.

National Association for the Advancement of Colored People, Victor Valley Branch. ***Certificate of Recognition for Outstanding Support***. October 4, 1991. NAACP Awards Banquet Guest Speaker.

San Bernardino Black Culture Foundation. ***Black History Queen***. 1992.

The Phylaxis Society. ***Recognition of Dedication***. 1997.

Kiwanis Club of East San Bernardino. ***Certificate of***

Appreciation. December 8, 1997. Guest Speaker; "Recognition of Your Address".

St. Paul A.M.E. Church. ***Certificate of Award and Recognition for Outstanding Achievement***. May 31, 1998.

St. Paul African Methodist Episcopal Church. ***Blessings Award***. For being a Blessing in so many lives. October 2000. Reverend Alvin Smith.

The Rite 33rd Degree Prince Hall Masons. ***Grateful Appreciation***. January 13, 2001. Guest Speaker at annual banquet.

Black Rose Culture Foundation. ***2003 Black Rose Award***. 2003.

St. Paul African Methodist Episcopal Church. ***Sincere Appreciation***. June 8, 2003. Speaker at the Scholarship Luncheon.

San Bernardino-Riverside Alumni Chapter Delta Sigma Theta Sorority. ***Outstanding Community Contributions and Economic Development***. May 20, 2006.

PAL Center Upward Bound Program. ***For Her Dream, Her Vision, Her Dedication, Her Guidance and Support***. August 5, 2008.

National Association of Women Business Owners. Inland

Empire. ***Legacy Nominee***.

PUBLICATIONS

Hampton-Henry, Mildred Dalton. ***The Concerns of Black Re-entry Females Selected North Central Association Graduate Schools***. A Dissertation. Southern Illinois University at Carbondale August 1983.

Hampton-Henry, Mildred Dalton. ***Setting Up A Responsive Guidance Program In A Middle School***. The Guidance Clinic. Parker Publishing Company. New York, 1979.

Hampton-Henry, Mildred Dalton. ***Black Entry Females: Their Concerns and Needs***. Journal of the National Association for Women Deans, Administrators, and Counselors. Volume 48, No. 4. Washington, D.C., 1985.

Hampton-Henry, Mildred Dalton. ***The Resource Student: A Copout or a Challenge***. Empowerment for Change. African American Church. Atlanta, GA

Made in the USA
Monee, IL
25 July 2022

6f4e1578-8cc6-427d-9139-3b2380f47dcdR01